Welcome to
Senior's Edition
iPad

The iPad is one of the most intriguing pieces of technology on the planet. Allowing you to have extreme portability while undertaking an incredible number of day-to-day tasks, it acts as a camera, movable media hub, games console and much more, all through a user-friendly and dynamic interface. It wouldn't be an exaggeration to say that the iPad has changed the way that many people go about their lives. So, now you have your hands on this life-changing device. With this revised edition, you can benefit from all that the iPad has to offer with the new iOS 8. From iCloud to the iPad's improved multitasking, Senior's Edition: iPad will cover all you need to know about your device and its interface. Enjoy the book!

Senior's Edition
iPad

Imagine Publishing Ltd
Richmond House
33 Richmond Hill
Bournemouth
Dorset BH2 6EZ
☎ +44 (0) 1202 586200
Website: www.imagine-publishing.co.uk
Twitter: @Books_Imagine
Facebook: www.facebook.com/ImagineBookazines

Publishing Director
Aaron Asadi

Head of Design
Ross Andrews

Production Editor
Jen Neal

Senior Art Editor
Greg Whitaker

Art Editor
Ali Innes

Photographer
James Sheppard

Printed by
William Gibbons, 26 Planetary Road, Willenhall, West Midlands, WV13 3XT

Distributed in the UK, Eire & the Rest of the World by:
Marketforce, Blue Fin Building, 110 Southwark Street, London, SE1 0SU
Tel 0203 148 3300 www.marketforce.co.uk

Distributed in Australia by:
Network Services (a division of Bauer Media Group), Level 21 Civic Tower, 66-68 Goulburn Street,
Sydney, New South Wales 2000, Australia Tel +61 2 8667 5288

Part of the
iCreate™
bookazine series

IMAGINE
PUBLISHING

Contents

18 Accessibility features

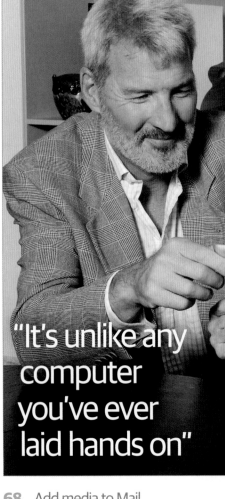

"It's unlike any computer you've ever laid hands on"

Apps

Helpdesk

The next step

Introducing the iPad

Let's explore the iPad's basic features

The iPad is unlike any computer you've ever laid your hands on. For one thing, there's no intermediary between you and what you're trying to do; on a regular computer, you have to learn to manipulate a pointing device like a mouse or trackpad to move a cursor on the screen so you can achieve what you need to do. On the iPad, you're already an expert manipulator since you just use your fingers directly on the screen to move and affect what you see. If you know how to point, you know how to use an iPad, and that's the truly exciting thing about this device: it makes personal computing truly personal.

But despite its friendliness, it's still a complex piece of hardware and you'll need to know a little about what makes it tick: how you turn it on, for instance, and what functions its few buttons offer. And what about all the other controls embedded in the software? How can you use its many features to the fullest?

We will endeavour to show you all this over the next few pages, helping you feel comfortable with the device so you can hit the ground running in no time at all.

Browsing

As soon as you've connected to your local wireless network, the iPad is ready to be an internet browsing device. In fact, when Apple's engineers were first experimenting with touch-screen devices, the original idea was a tablet designed for web browsing. As a result, going online is a very polished experience and a joy to use. Like all other apps on the iPad, tapping on the Safari icon fills the screen with that program's content, removing any other distractions. You can then browse the web with your fingers. If you're familiar with Safari on your Mac or PC, you'll feel right at home – there's even a Google search field. Tapping on it increases its size and reveals the keyboard so you can type what you're looking for. The same applies for the address field if you know exactly where you want to go. Thanks to iCloud, you can sync your Mac's bookmarks to your iPad, right down to the Bookmark Bar.

Navigating a webpage is easy: you flick your finger up, down, left or right to see other parts of the page. If you want to focus on a specific section, double-tap on it to zoom in on it. There are other browsers on the App Store, such as Google Chrome and Opera Mini, so have a look to see if one suits your needs better than Safari.

Communication

Browsing the web isn't the only thing you need to do online. For one thing, you need to check your emails and the iPad's got you covered there as well, thanks to the Mail application. With it, you can set up as many accounts as you need. Just like Mail on your Mac, you have a universal inbox where all your messages, irrespective of which address they were sent to, can be accessed, read and replied to. You can also organise your messages, making it easier to keep track of a conversation.

When it comes to social networking, you can either make use of Safari – aside from its games, Facebook works very well in the iPad's web browser (the games don't work because they rely on Adobe's Flash platform, which isn't compatible with the iPad, iPhone

"Chances are someone may already have designed a great solution that fits your exact needs"

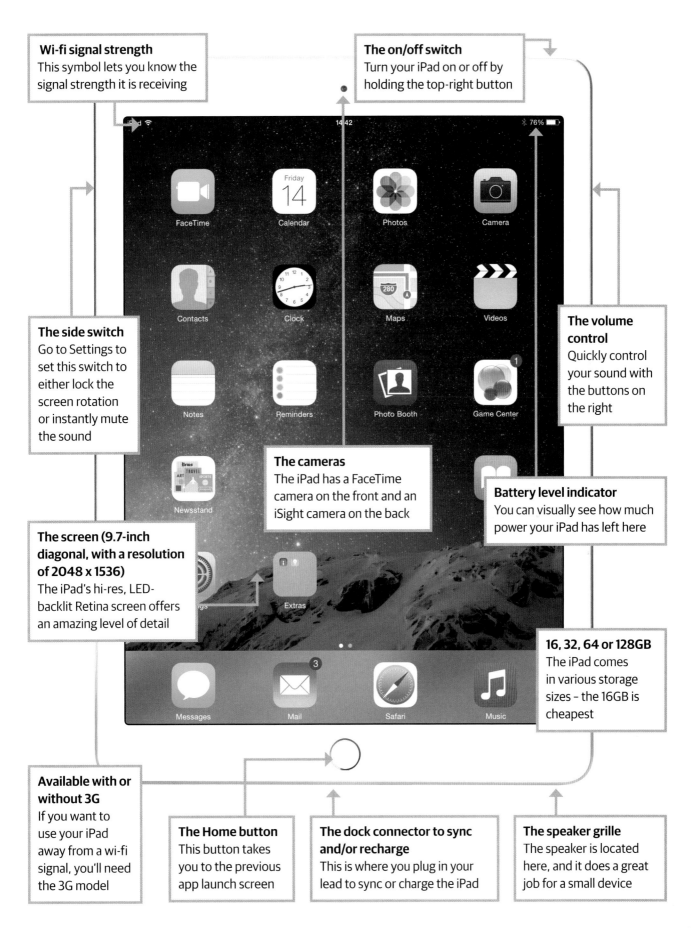

Wi-fi signal strength
This symbol lets you know the signal strength it is receiving

The on/off switch
Turn your iPad on or off by holding the top-right button

The side switch
Go to Settings to set this switch to either lock the screen rotation or instantly mute the sound

The volume control
Quickly control your sound with the buttons on the right

The cameras
The iPad has a FaceTime camera on the front and an iSight camera on the back

Battery level indicator
You can visually see how much power your iPad has left here

The screen (9.7-inch diagonal, with a resolution of 2048 x 1536)
The iPad's hi-res, LED-backlit Retina screen offers an amazing level of detail

16, 32, 64 or 128GB
The iPad comes in various storage sizes – the 16GB is cheapest

Available with or without 3G
If you want to use your iPad away from a wi-fi signal, you'll need the 3G model

The Home button
This button takes you to the previous app launch screen

The dock connector to sync and/or recharge
This is where you plug in your lead to sync or charge the iPad

The speaker grille
The speaker is located here, and it does a great job for a small device

or iPod touch) – or look for the dedicated iPad apps, like Facebook and Twitter, at the App Store. These have been integrated into iOS so that you can tweet and share from within a host of default Apple apps.

Other applications, like Skype, enable you to enjoy full-screen video calls on your iPad with other people who don't necessarily own an Apple device, or there's the default FaceTime app for people who do.

Photos

If you see images on the web you'd like to keep, you can easily save them to your Photos application by tapping and holding on one and choosing 'Save Image' from the popover menu. But that's not the only use of that particular program. Thanks to iOS's iCloud feature, you can activate Photo Stream so that any pictures taken on your iPad or iPhone are automatically pushed to all of your iOS devices and Macs running OS X 10.7.2 or higher.

You can also dispense with a bigger computer entirely by getting the iPad Camera Connection Kit and transfer photos and videos from any compatible digital stills camera straight to your iPad library – after which Photo Stream will make them instantly available on all of your devices, automatically and completely wirelessly.

Once there, you can browse through your photos, post them online or send them to friends and family. If you want to upload them to Facebook or Twitter, you can do this via the Photo app. Select the image you want to use and tap the Share button to see the options. You can also set it as wallpaper.

First steps
Getting acquainted with your iPad
Turn on
When an iPad's screen is off, your device is either asleep or shut down

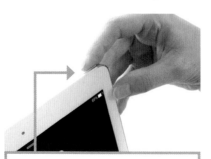 

01 To turn the device on when it has been fully turned off, press the On/Off button, top right of the device.

02 If it's in Sleep mode, you can also press the Home button to bring your iPad back to life.

Sleep mode
You may be putting your iPad to sleep quite often

01 You need to make use of one of your iPad's few physical buttons for this: the On/Off one, at the top right of the device.

02 Press and release it once for the screen to go dark and become unresponsive to any touch input.

Turn off
To turn your iPad off, check out the following steps

01 Press and hold on its On/Off button for up to five seconds. The screen will dim and a red slider will appear.

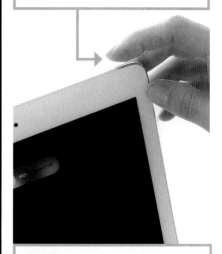

02 Move that red slider from left to right to confirm that you wish to shut the iPad down.

Change volume

Depending on what you're doing, you can change the volume in various ways

01 Use the physical buttons, top of the iPad's right edge. The top one increases the volume and the bottom one lowers it.

02 If you're watching a movie or listening to music, you'll find a slider on the screen to achieve the same result.

Rotation lock

Here's how to stop the screen from rotating each time you change position

01 Go to Settings and, under 'General', set the 'Use Side Switch to:' option to 'Lock Rotation' and then slide the side switch.

02 If your side switch is set to Mute, double-tap the Home button, scroll to the right and then tap the rotation lock icon.

Brightness

If the screen is too light or dark for your tastes, you can alter it like so...

01 Tap on the Settings app and select the 'Brightness & Wallpaper' menu. Use the slider to lower or raise the brightness.

02 Double-click the Home button and slide the new bar of icons to the right. You'll find a brightness slider there as well.

Unlock

Once you've woken your iPad up, you'll be graced with its Lock screen

01 To gain access, use the slider at the bottom of the screen to unlock your iPad.

02 If you have set a password, you will have to type it in before you can proceed any further.

Mute

To mute the volume of the iPad, you have two options...

01 If you have the side switch set to Mute, slide it down to mute your iPad.

02 Press and hold the volume-down button. After two seconds, it'll be muted.

Charge

Recharging the iPad is a simple matter

01 Unless your computer is recent enough, there won't be enough power from its USB port to charge the iPad.

02 For a faster, more efficient charge, it's best to use the bundled power adaptor instead.

Sync

To back up or transfer files, you need to sync

Sync with iCloud
Go to page 30 for this syncing option

01 Use the bundled cable to connect your iPad via one of your computer's USB ports.

02 It will launch iTunes and the backup and syncing process will by default be totally automatic.

Music

It wouldn't be an Apple device if it didn't let you listen to your music, but although iTunes is responsible for almost everything media-related on your Mac, the iPad has broken those features into multiple apps designed for specific purposes. For instance, you can purchase new music using the iTunes application, but if you want to listen to albums you currently own, then you have to use the Music app. From there, you gain access to your songs, podcasts and audiobooks. If you want to watch a music video, however, you'll need to take a trip to the Videos app.

But iTunes isn't the only way you can listen to music on your iPad. There are other programs that let you stream songs directly from the internet and, just like the Music application, they can be used to listen to music in the background while you work in another program on your iPad. If you're in the UK, make sure you check out Spotify, while US readers should take a look at Pandora.

Watching

Although it's no substitute for your widescreen television, when you're away from your couch, the iPad makes for a surprisingly good TV. Due to its size, it's much better than an iPhone or iPod touch and its built-in speaker is good enough to allow the device to be shared, but what can you watch on it? Well, anything you've bought or rented from the iTunes Store will work on your iPad:

you can transfer movies, TV shows, podcasts and music videos and they'll all play flawlessly on your portable device.

You could also convert your existing DVD collection into iTunes-compatible files; but in order to achieve this, you'd need desktop computer programs like HandBrake which are designed to transform your films and episodes into compatible files ready for you to enjoy on your iPad. This can be a time-consuming process, so why not try the brilliant television services such as the BBC iPlayer and Sky Go, both of which offer

catch-up services? The Sky+ app lets UK viewers record programmes remotely to watch on their Sky+ in-home boxes. The EyeTV application also lets you watch live television as long as you're within range of your wireless signal.

Entertainment

There's been a lot of talk about the iPad (and other iOS devices) not being compatible with Adobe's Flash, but this is actually less of a

iTunes The desktop software explored

Where can I get it?

■ Point your browser towards www.itunes.com and click on the 'Download iTunes' button, somewhere on the page.

What is iTunes?

■ It's a program designed by Apple and the purpose was to transfer your CD collection onto your Mac, catalogue your songs and transfer them to a compatible MP3 player.

Why do I need it?

■ Because iTunes evolved over the years to accommodate more than music – movies, TV shows, podcasts and more. Now it's a great way to transfer anything to your iPad.

Why is it not included on a CD?

■ Apple now assumes that broadband is ubiquitous, and that way the company can make sure that you'll be using the very latest version

available as opposed to one that could have been released ages ago.

It's installed. Now what?

■ Double-click on its icon to open it and agree to the licence agreement. You can convert your music CDs to iPad-compatible files or purchase new songs, movies and shows from the iTunes Store.

What happens when I connect my iPad to my computer?

■ iTunes will take over your iPad and you will be asked not to disconnect it while the syncing process is taking place. Your iPad's data will be backed up and your media will be synchronised between your devices.

How do I cancel the sync?

■ When your iPad is connected to iTunes, its screen informs you not to disconnect it. However, there is a slider at the bottom which you can use to cancel the sync should you need to. Note that your iPad will not be fully backed up if you do this.

---

problem than you might think. For one thing, although you won't be able to go to **www.youtube.com** and watch videos via the Safari internet browser, there's a dedicated YouTube application which enables you to do just that instead. You can watch clips, comment on them and do pretty much everything you'd expect to be able to do, but you will need to download this from the App Store since Apple removed the built-in YouTube app from iOS 6.

Other video sites, like Vimeo, offer iPad-compatible versions of their videos, so you can watch those straight from your web browser.

But being entertained is much more than just passively watching something on the screen; you can also use your iPad to read the latest bestseller or enjoy a timeless classic. The two major programs that allow you to do this are Apple's own iBooks and Amazon's Kindle. Both are also compatible with the iPod, iPhone and Mac (Apple has now included the iBooks app as a default app on your iPad with the release of iOS 8), so you can stop reading on the iPad and carry on with another device if you'd like. Not all titles are available in digital form, but there's still plenty of choice.

Games

When it comes to games, you will be spoilt for choice. There are so many available to download, both free and paid-for. You can spend hours getting immersed in an adventure story (thank goodness for the iPad's excellent battery life), or just use it to while away a few minutes of your time every now and again.

The obvious choices are there, like arcade-style games such as The

Introduction

very convenient and enables you to work between the two systems.

But the iPad can go a lot further than this. For one thing, the iWork suite is available for it as a separate purchase. You obviously won't get all the features that you've grown accustomed to with the Mac's versions, but for a first attempt at creating a business suite that's controlled by touch, it's remarkable what you can do with these apps and you'll be designing newsletters, filling in spreadsheets and creating presentations in next to no time at all.

If you need compatibility with Microsoft Word and iWork's conversion layer isn't good enough, take a look at Byte²'s Office² HD. It's not as attractive as the iWork suite, but it lets you create native Word (both .doc and .docx) and Excel (.xls) documents on your iPad for a very reasonable price.

"The iPad is a very powerful machine capable of doing almost anything a computer can"

Incident and Fruit Ninja HD; plus adventure games like Hero of Sparta 2 and Max; strategy games like Cut the Rope and Angry Birds; and role-playing games like Aralon and Galaxy on Fire 2. There's even an iPad version of Farmville.

But none of these offers anything new from what you could achieve on a regular computer. What sets the iPad apart from other platforms is that its screen is large enough that it can be easily viewed by multiple people at the same time. As a result, it's become a natural digital alternative to board games, making playing on a computer a much more social experience with people in the same room as you, just like the good old days. Make sure you check out titles like WarChess, Carcassonne, Scrabble, Monopoly and The Game

Of Life. Whatever your tastes, though, the iPad has them covered.

Office work

The iPad isn't just a device to browse the web, watch videos and play games, however. Many people classify it as just a media consumption device, but it's in fact a very powerful machine capable of doing almost anything a regular computer can. It comes with a Notes program which you can use to jot down a few ideas, lists or even the beginning of a draft letter. That application syncs with your emails and you can access those documents in your Mac's Mail program, which is

Productivity

As for other productivity programs, Calendar stores all your appointments and syncs with Calendar on your Mac – as long as you have activated your free iOS iCloud account. The same applies for the Contacts app, even preserving all your groups so you'll feel right at home on your device.

Surprisingly, the iPad doesn't come with a calculator application built-in to the system, but this can be easily remedied with a short visit to the App Store. Just type in 'Calculator' in the search field to find enough free and paid options to satisfy your needs. Another feature missing

App Store A vital part of the iPad explained

What's all this talk about apps? Do I need them?
■ Apps are programs that run on a computer, like your browser or word processor. They increase your device's functionality and you should definitely browse through them to see if there's anything you might like.

Where do I get these apps?
■ Straight from the App Store, which you can access from iTunes

or the iPad app. You might find some websites showcasing various programs, but you can only get them from the App Store.

Can I only get them from my computer?
■ No: there's a program called 'App Store' on your iPad. From there, you can gain access to the entire store as well, although you will need to be within range of a wi-fi network, unless of course you own a 3G-capable iPad.

What if I'm just browsing? Can I find stuff easily?
■ Of course: the App Store is designed to help you buy. As a result, you can look through various lists like top sellers, top free apps, staff recommendations, and so on.

Is there any trial software?
■ Not as such, but many developers have 'lite' or 'free' versions of their applications. These offer limited functionality or a few sample levels

if it's a game. If you like what you see, you can then purchase the full program and delete the lite copy.

It's all a bit of a jumble; can I narrow my search down?
■ The App Store is broken into 20 categories, each with its own top sellers list. You can narrow your search by focusing on a single one.

How can I ask questions or get help from the developer?
■ At the bottom of every app description is a link to the developer's website. More often than not, you'll find a contact email address there, which you can use to write to the developer or company and get the help you need.

Why does my App Store icon have red numbers on it?
■ These badges are there to show you that your apps have been updated and that you can get those new versions for free directly from the App Store's Updates section.

from the iPad is any possibility of using it like an external drive, but the fantastic advantage of the iPad (and any device powered by the iOS software) is the huge number of developers working on it. As a result, someone's come up with a way of achieving just that, thanks to an application called 'USB Disk Pro for iPad' (a free version is also available under the title of 'USB Disk for iPad'), so you can easily use your iPad like an external portable hard drive.

Chances are, whatever it is you're looking for, someone may already have designed a solution that fits your exact needs.

Creative apps
That's exactly the case with graphic design applications. Adobe, maker of the mighty Photoshop, has only dipped its toes into the iPad, but other, smaller developers have jumped at the opportunity that this new platform offers them and there's a wealth of programs that allow you to design with your fingers anything you used to need a mouse or a graphic tablet for in the past.

The beauty of the iPad is that these programs are so cheap compared to those you'd find on a Mac or Windows PC that trying some out isn't as financially crippling as it can be on other platforms.

You're bound to find the right program that matches your abilities. If you're artistically inclined, have a look at SketchBook Pro, Freeform or Brushes. If you're looking for programs that help you transform pictures into visually stunning works of art, explore Artist's Touch or the PhotoArtistaHD series of applications. If you fancy more specific effects, consider

Accessories

Enrich your hardware with some great kit...

Keyboard The iPad is great for many things, although some people still struggle with typing using the device. You can get around this by purchasing an Apple Wireless Keyboard and then pairing it with your iPad via Bluetooth

Protective films Even if you prefer your iPad to be without a case, you should consider a film to protect its most important part: the screen. Some high-quality ones not only protect it from accidental scratches, they actually make it easier to clean and fingerprints don't stick as easily as they would on a bare piece of glass

Case Getting an iPad case is essential if you wish to protect your investment and they come in many styles. Most can display your iPad in portrait or landscape orientation and can be supported at a variety of angles for browsing, working or watching movies

Smartcase This device will enthral you for hours with its ingenuity. With the clever use of magnets, you can, literally, sling this cover at your iPad and it will auto-align to sit perfectly across the screen of your device for supreme protection. What's more, when you pull it back, your device will automatically wake up

Styluses Controlling objects with your fingers undoubtedly feels more natural, but a stylus can be great for precision work. A few companies have created such devices that work very well with the iPad's capacitive screen

"It's undeniable how truly amazing it is to be able to scroll through a map and effortlessly zoom in and out of a location using your fingers alone"

Apple TV Your iPad is a great device to play all of your downloaded movies, videos and music, but if you want to broadcast them on a bigger stage then Apple TV is perfect. This device transforms your TV into a viewing portal for all of your Apple content and it does so wirelessly – you just sit back and control your evening's entertainment from your iPad

Speakers The iPad's mono speaker may be surprisingly good for an item of its size, but it's really not sufficient to enjoy your media to the fullest. Thankfully, there are many external speakers available to improve the experience. They either connect via its mini-jack, the dock connector or even wirelessly via Bluetooth

TypeDrawing or Glow Painter Pro HD. Those of you missing iPhoto's adjustment tools should purchase TouchUp, and your grandchildren will love Drawing Pad.

Maps

All of the above can be achieved whether you own a Wi-Fi-only iPad or one capable of connecting to a 3G network (ie one that hooks up to a mobile phone network and hence gets you online wherever you have coverage – for a price). If you've decided to invest in a 3G-capable iPad, the capabilities of your machine are greatly extended since you'll be able to browse, check you emails or even play online games wherever you might be.

There's also the added advantage of being able to use the Maps application to help you navigate to your desired location. Apple replaced the Google Maps app with its own for iOS 7, but it does give turn-by-turn directions and hooks into the Siri function too.

You may get tired of hearing how 'magical' the iPad is, but it's undeniable how truly amazing it is to be able to scroll through a map and effortlessly zoom in and out of a location using your fingers alone. The program is incredibly responsive and the only limitation you'll experience will be due to your internet's bandwidth. It illustrates just how wonderful using this device truly

is. There are also other map apps available, so check out the App Store to find one that suits you.

Kids

The iPad is an amazing learning tool no matter what your age is; there's even a dedicated section called 'Apps for Kids' in the App Store, where you can get interactive books like Winnie the Pooh or The Cat in the Hat, programs that teach you how to read and write or even understand the world around you, help you play music, draw... pretty much anything you can imagine.

Older children haven't been left out either: MathBoard is a fantastic program designed to help you perfect your algebra. You can even set which calculations to work on and how difficult they should be. There are also many apps designed to keep kids entertained, such as wordsearch apps like WordSeek HD and much more.

If you're interested in space, you can learn everything you need to know thanks to programs like Solar Walk or Solar System for iPad, and the little ones can keep up with their older siblings with iLearn Solar System HD. If it's dinosaurs you're after, check out Ultimate Dinopedia, and if you want to explore all the elements that make up our universe, be sure to look for The Elements – there's even a British edition with UK English spelling.

Make your iPad easier to use

An iPad can be the perfect computer for anyone who finds traditional devices out of reach

Accessibility is a hallmark of all Apple products, but for those who do not need them they are hidden away, which can mean a lack of awareness. A quick look in the Accessibility settings, which are available in the Settings app under the General option, will offer most of the options that can help you overcome physical restrictions to make the most of your iPad. They are all turned off by default, but once the setup process is complete the experience changes. The iPad can speak back any action you undertake so that you always know where you are, the screen can be zoomed in to a hugely magnified view and text can be set to the level which is perfect for your needs. Hardware buttons need never be touched thanks to AssistiveTouch and the sound can be sent to just one earphone speaker to lessen conflict with hearing aids. Whatever your requirements, the iPad has every accessibility function you need.

Interact with ease

VoiceOver is an ingenious feature which is designed to help those who have any form of vision impairment. It speaks as you interact with the iPad and does a lot more than just read text that is on screen. It will read text from web pages and documents when a paragraph is tapped and this alone can bring a world of information to anyone, but the main benefit lies in its ability to let you use the iPad in exactly the same way as anyone else; tap a button on screen and it is described aloud, double-tap it and the action is completed. It can be activated from the Settings app by choosing 'General' followed by 'Accessibility'. Here you can also change the speed of the voice feedback and many other settings.

■ A paragraph of text that is tapped will be spoken immediately by the iPad

■ Select Braille devices are compatible with the iPad and connect using Bluetooth

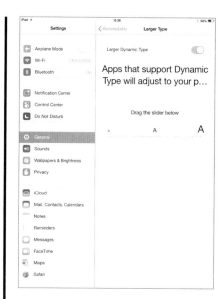

Get larger text

■ The Large Text feature offers a variety of text sizes from 20 point all the way up to 56 point. Go to the Settings app, then General, Accessibility, and choose 'Large Text'. The text is displayed in scale to let you choose the most comfortable.

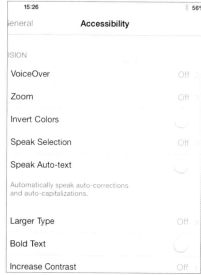

Speak Selection

■ Speak Selection, available via Settings, General, and Accessibility, lets you set up the iPad to offer a 'Speak' option when you select text. You can set the speed and also choose from a huge range of dialects.

> "VoiceOver is an ingenious feature designed to help those who have any form of vision impairment"

Simple keyboard shortcuts

Split keyboard

01 With the keyboard in view, hold your finger on the bottom-right keyboard icon and then select 'Split' from the menu that pops up. You can now type with your thumbs and hold the device with two hands.

Accents

02 To create an accent over any letter, hold your finger on the letter and then slide it to one of the accents that pops above it. Every accent that you might need for your language will be included automatically.

Caps lock

03 Tapping a Shift key (the arrow) lets you insert a capital letter and the key will show a blue outline. If you double-tap a Shift key, it changes to a white arrow in a blue icon to signify that caps lock is enabled.

Quick apostrophes

04 By default, the iPad's keyboard has the apostrophe button on the Numbers keyboard. However, if you hold down the exclamation mark key, you can access a quick apostrophe on the Letters one.

Punctuation

05 You may need to type unusual punctuation. Tap the numbers key (bottom-left) and then hold your finger on any punctuation key. Under some you will find all of the obscure and rare punctuation that you need.

Use simple gestures

 AssistiveTouch is designed to make complex manual interaction with an iPad a thing of the past. Once enabled in the Accessibility options you will see a small transparent dot on the screen at all times. It is unobtrusive and never gets in the way of what you are doing, but a simple tap gives you immediate access to every hardware function you need. It has options to mimic pressing the Home button and activating Siri, but it is the 'Device' and 'Favourites' options that truly stand out. You can set up favourites for your most used gestures that are tricky to perform and the device icon includes tasks such as changing

■ The most often used system functions are a couple of taps away with AssistiveTouch

the volume and rotating the screen. In effect it removes the need for hardware keys on the iPad and brings them all together under a small window which only appears when you need it. You can even create your own gestures.

"It makes complex manual interaction with an iPad a thing of the past"

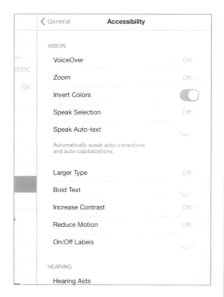

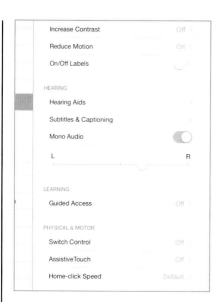

Invert colours

■ The ability to invert the colours on screen and to make a negative photo effect can make reading much easier in some circumstances. In the usual Accessibility settings page simply tap the option and switch the icon to 'On'. Tap it again to turn it off.

Read subtitles

■ In the Accessibility settings, tap on 'Subtitles & Captioning'. Now change Closed Captioning to 'On' and when you next watch a TV show or movie that supports the facility, you will see the subtitles on screen throughout. It's simple to set up.

Get mono audio

■ In the Accessibility settings, you will see a 'Hearing' section. Tap the icon to turn it on and now you can use the slider to decide which side you would like the mono audio to sound. This is particularly useful when hearing aids are being used.

Zoom in

The Zoom feature in the Accessibility options of the Settings app, which requires just one tap to enable, lets you increase the size of everything on screen in a variety of ways. To zoom in, all you have to do is double-tap three fingers on screen and do the same to zoom out again.

You move around the screen using three fingers instead of one and can also set the zoom to any level you like by double-tapping with three fingers and then sliding them until the appropriate level is reached. This means that you can choose how exactly the zoom is set for each app or task and thus it gives you all of the control you require in every situation

you encounter on an iPad. The fact that it can be turned off easily is another bonus – for many partially

sighted people it could prove to be the most useful accessibility feature of all.

Setting up

Get your iPad up and running with these easy-to-follow tips

"Just got an iPad? We'll guide you through the process of setting up your device"

Activate and register your iPad

Just got an iPad? We'll guide you through the process of setting up your device and registering it to your Apple ID

With trembling hands and a giddy sensation in your stomach, you unpack your new iPad from its box and are ready to activate it and start using it to enhance your life. But whereas previously you would have to have had a computer to plug your iPad into to start the setup process, since iOS 5 (the current is iOS 8) you no longer need to tether your device to a computer and the entire setup can be carried out independently, which makes it a quick and easy process.

All you have to do is connect your new device to a power source and then press the Sleep/Wake button, which is situated on the top of your iPad. This will bring up a generic iPad lock screen with a slider at the bottom. Tap and hold on the slider with your index finger and swipe it to the right to unlock the device and the next series of screens will guide you through the setup process. In this tutorial we will take you through each stage of the process and explain what each screen is asking you to do.

Activation Prepare your iPad

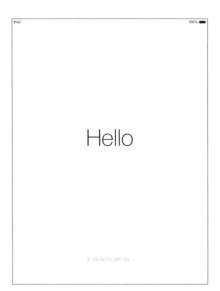

01 When you switch on your iPad for the very first time you will be presented with a plain-looking lock screen with a slider at the bottom. Tap and hold the slider and swipe it to the right to unlock the iPad.

02 On the first two set-up screens you will need to choose a native language for your device and also choose your region so that the content of the iTunes and App Stores can be set accordingly. Tap your preference.

03 Your iPad chiefly relies on a Wi-FI network to be able to connect to the internet and fuel a wealth of different services. If you are within range of a Wi-FI network then it will be detected. Enter the password and connect

Your Settings
Your first port of call should be the Settings app. Tap on this to start modifying and customising certain aspects of your device

Your apps
A selection of Apple apps are built in to the operating system and will appear on your Home screen as standard. Tap on an icon to launch the app

Your Dock
The Dock is a row of app icons in a strip at the bottom of the screen. This Dock is present no matter which of your screens you're on and should be used for your most-used apps

Adding apps
The Dock contains four apps as standard but you can add an extra one by tapping and holding on an icon until it starts to shake and then dragging it with your finger into the Dock

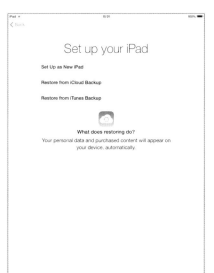

04 Location Services allows apps to gather and use data indicating your approximate location, which can be useful. Enable or disable it here. You can activate it later from Settings>Privacy>Location Services.

05 The next screen presents you with three options. You can either set up the device as a new iPad, which is what you'll be doing, or restore it from previous settings backed up to your iCloud or iTunes.

06 You'll need your own Apple ID to enjoy the main features of your iPad, such as being able to download apps, music and videos and back up and sync your data and settings with iCloud. Sign in or create a new one.

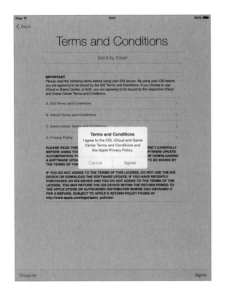

07 After signing in, you will be presented with a screen of Terms and Conditions that relate to all aspects of your iPad and the services that you will be using, such as iCloud, Game Center and so on.

08 If you wish to use iCloud, use your Apple ID to sign into your free account. iCloud lets you access music, photos, contacts and more on all of your devices automatically and is well worth using.

09 If you misplace your iPad then Find My iPad will help you locate it on a map, play a sound or display a message. You can activate this service to sync the location of your device with iCloud.

10 The FaceTime app lets you speak face-to-face with people using your iPad's built-in camera, while iMessage provides free messaging. Enter your email address or phone number to use the services.

11 Next you will be presented with Create A Passcode. Here, you can enter a four-digit passcode that will be used to secure your iPad. The code will need to be entered every time you unlock your device and prevents others from using it

12 At this stage of the process you can choose to enable Siri, your iOS-based personal assistant. You can ask Siri questions or give commands in plain English to access and open apps, information, perform tasks and much more.

The categories
All of the categories to which the Settings apply will be presented in a list on the left-hand side of the screen. Tap an option to bring up its individual screen of settings

All about your iPad
By tapping on the 'About' option in the 'General' section, you can get in-depth info on your device, such as the serial number, capacity and the amount of space that your various apps and media take up

Side Switch
The switch on the side of your device can be used for muting sound or locking your screen rotation. The latter is very useful and you can assign it from the 'General' Settings section

Software Update
By tapping on the 'Software Update' option in the 'General' section your device will be able to find and update your iOS, without the need to connect your device to a computer

13 Apple likes to keep track of how its products are performing, so this screen allows you to send diagnostic data straight to Apple for their records. Opt for 'Don't Send' to keep your information private.

14 Congratulations! You have now worked your way through the entire set-up process. A screen will confirm the process is complete, so what are you waiting for? Tap on the 'Get Started' button and get using your iPad.

15 You'll be presented with your home screen, so start tapping on icons to launch apps and find your way around, experimenting with the gestures needed to operate your new device. Going into Settings will let you personalise your device.t

Change Settings to suit you

The Settings app is the epicentre of your iPad. Here you can customise everything from how apps work to the feel of the display

On the first page of the iPad screen is an app called Settings. This controls how your iPad works, allows individual apps to be configured and sets the look and feel of the screens. With it, you can enforce security, log on to Wi-Fi networks, save battery power, add signatures to emails, configure the web browser Safari to use specific search engines and much, much more. It is, perhaps, the most important app on your iPad, and

one you will come to use a lot. Learn what it has to offer and how you can change or configure things and you will take control of the iPad to make it work the way you want it to.

In this tutorial we are going to introduce you to some of the key features within Settings – the ones that you may want to

check out straight away to get yourself acquainted to the system and personalise it for your own preferences. More specific tutorials will follow to show you functions in more depth, but for now, let's delve into the nerve centre of this incredible piece of kit. this incredible piece of kit.

"Learn what the Settings have to offer and make the iPad work the way you want"

Settings Work your way around the iPad's control system

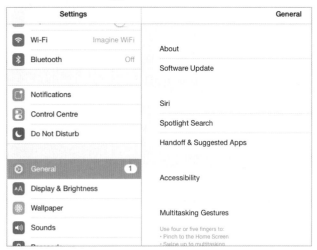 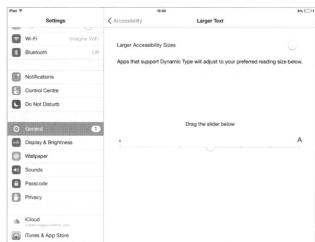

01 Turn your iPad on and slide the bar across to unlock it. The Settings app is on the first screen. Tap on it to launch. There are a number of parameters but you'll find a lot of useful things to tweak in the 'General' section. If this isn't automatically selected, tap on it now.

02 Within the General settings you can set up Siri, adjust the text size, make your device easier to use if you have an impairment, determine the function of the side switch and set a passcode lock on your device (if you didn't do it during the initial setup process).

Wireless Updates

With iOS 7+ you no longer need to connect your iPad to a computer in order to update the system software. Just choose 'Software Update' to get the latest iOS (if available) beamed directly to your device

About Your iPad

Tapping on the About section will list all of your device's contents – including songs, videos, photos – divulge the storage capacity and how much space is free and more

Multitasking Gestures

Here you can turn on or off multitasking gestures, which allow you to use certain swipes of your fingers, such as swipe up, left, right or pinch with four or five fingers, to control your iPad

Lock Settings

Use Auto-Lock to decide how long you want the iPad to wait for inactivity before it locks, and use Passcode Lock if you want to set a password for when you first turn on your iPad

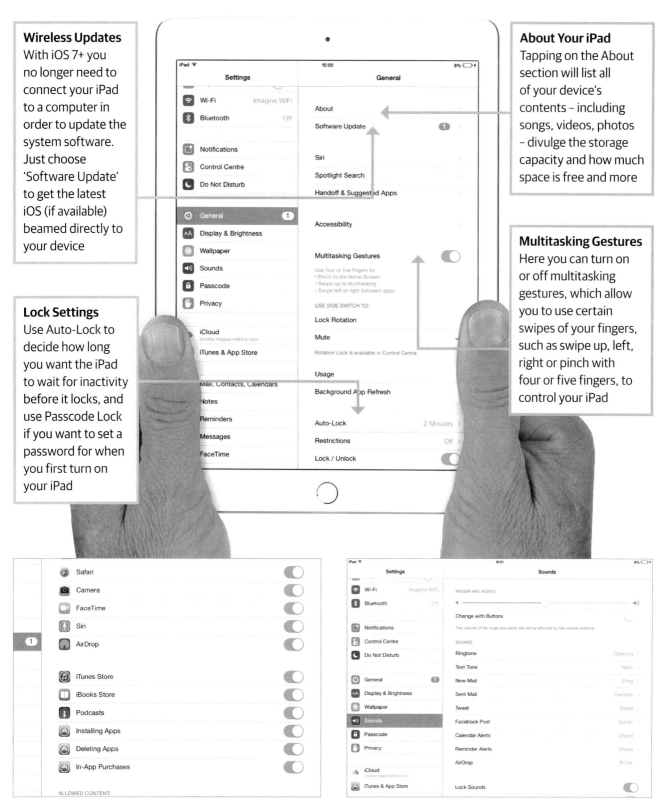

03 The 'General' section also has one of the most important settings options. Here you can turn off in-app purchases, access to iTunes and much more. Just tap 'Enable Restrictions' and you are prompted to set a passcode. Make it memorable.

04 The layout of the Settings screen has been changed slightly in iOS 8. Some settings, that were once part of other sections, now have their own standout section accessible from the list. Explore the list to get to grips with your device and what it can do.

Set up iCloud and start syncing

All of your documents can be moved wirelessly from device to device without you having to lift a finger

With iOS 5 came iCloud, a service from Apple that is so much more than just a hard drive in the sky. Free to all iOS users, iCloud automatically and securely stores your content so that it's always available on your iPad, iPhone, Mac… whatever Apple device you're using. Through iCloud you get full access to

your music, apps, photos and documents, and it also wirelessly syncs all of your emails, contacts and calendars to keep them up to date across all of your devices.

When you sign up for iCloud you get 5GB of free storage, which is plenty because all of your music, apps, books, and photos don't count against your free

storage. And seeing as your mail, documents, account info, settings and other app data don't use up much space, you'll find that your free quota goes a long way. You can now set up iCloud when you register, but if you opted not to or you registered your iPad before the iOS 5 update, follow these steps to set up iCloud now.

iCloud Setting up your personal iCloud

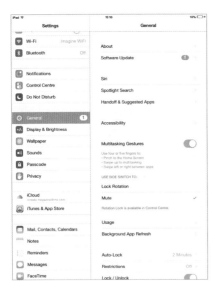

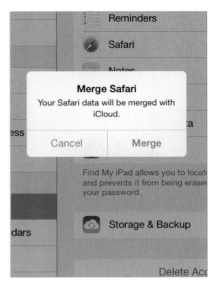

01 iCloud comes as part of iOS 5 and above. You can update via iTunes or the General tab in Settings. To manage your iCloud settings head to the iCloud tab of the menu. It will be in the section after General.

02 To activate your iCloud account you will need to log in using your Apple ID, which is the same email address and password that you use for your other services, such as iTunes and the App Store.

03 If you have already set up an iCloud account on another device, then you will be asked if you would like to merge data, such as calendars, with the data that exists on the iCloud. Choose 'Merge'.

Storage & Backup
You can select the option to automatically back up your iPad to iCloud under certain conditions and purchase more storage space if you need it

Your account
Your free iCloud is activated when you enter your Apple ID. This is the same email address and password that you use for other Apple services, such as iTunes

Delete Account
If you are upgrading your device and wish to disassociate your current iPad with an iCloud account then simply tap the 'Delete Account' option

Compatible apps
iCloud is integrated into a host of default Apple apps and works behind the scenes to make sure everything is synced across all your devices

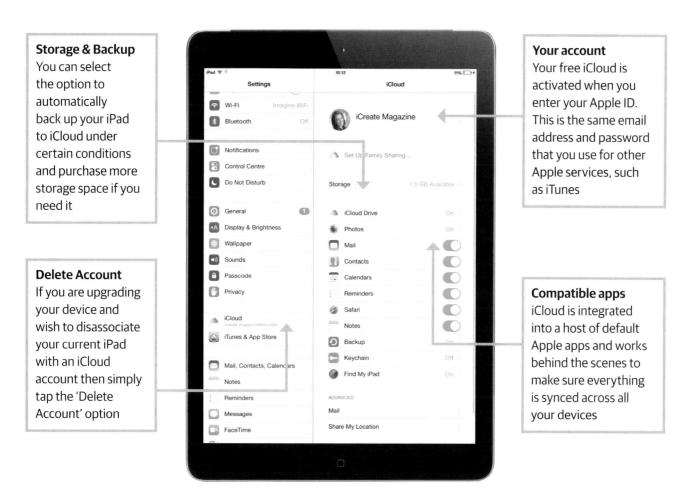

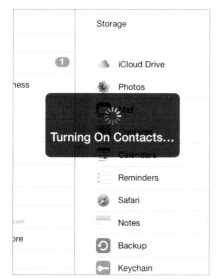

04 Select which of the apps utilise the service, such as Mail, Contacts, Calendar, Reminders, Safari Bookmarks, Notes, Photo Stream and Documents & Data. Move the sliders to activate the apps.

05 To get the most out of iCloud, click on the 'Store' section in Settings and then turn on 'Automatic Downloads' for Music, Apps and Books to download all new purchases from other devices straight to your iPad.

06 With iOS 8, your iPad now comes with a function called iCloud Drive. To activate this, tap on the iCloud Drive option under the iCloud menu. Follow the instructions on your screen to set it up.

Back up your iPad using iCloud

With iCloud, you can back up all of your important iPad data to your own virtual hard drive

Your iPad is like a bank vault where all kinds of important stuff is stored. So what happens if your iPad gets lost or goes awry? Nothing, that's what. Thanks to iCloud, all of your data is automatically backed up and kept safely in your own cloud storage space. When your iPad is connected to a power source and a Wi-FI network, all of your media, photos, videos, settings, app data and messages are backed up.

When you set up a new iOS device or need to restore the information on the one you already have, iCloud Backup does all the heavy lifting. All you have to do is ensure that your device is connected to Wi-FI, enter your Apple ID and all of your important data will appear on your device without you having to worry. As you will have read elsewhere in this book, the benefits of using iCloud are vast, and the way in which it goes about its business in the background without you having to worry shows how Apple want to make your life easier.

iCloud Activate iCloud and back up your data

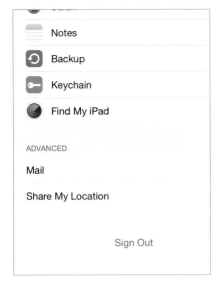

01 If you don't have the latest version of iOS, connect your device to your computer through iTunes and check to ensure you have the latest free software update installed on your device.

02 From your iPad's home screen, launch your Settings app and, in the left-hand column, you will see a new category called 'iCloud'. Tap on this option and then enter your Apple ID and password.

03 Once your personal iCloud has been set up and you have selected which apps you would like to sync, tap on the 'Backup' option found near the bottom of the list to begin the rest of the process.

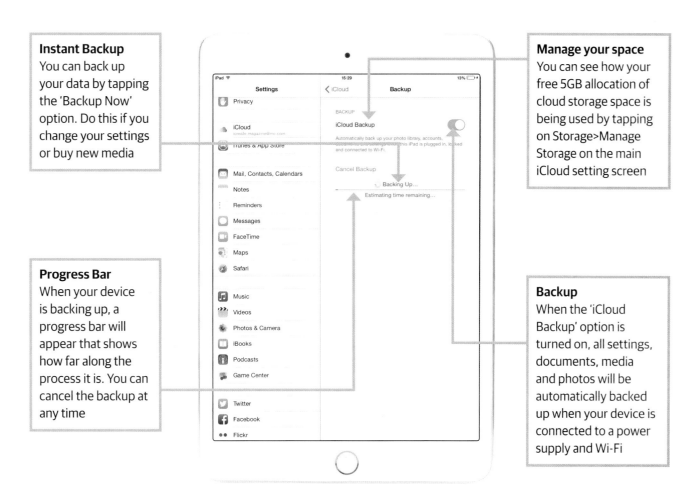

Instant Backup
You can back up your data by tapping the 'Backup Now' option. Do this if you change your settings or buy new media

Progress Bar
When your device is backing up, a progress bar will appear that shows how far along the process it is. You can cancel the backup at any time

Manage your space
You can see how your free 5GB allocation of cloud storage space is being used by tapping on Storage>Manage Storage on the main iCloud setting screen

Backup
When the 'iCloud Backup' option is turned on, all settings, documents, media and photos will be automatically backed up when your device is connected to a power supply and Wi-Fi

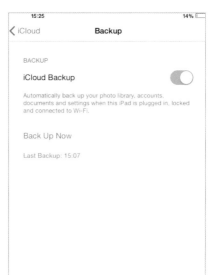

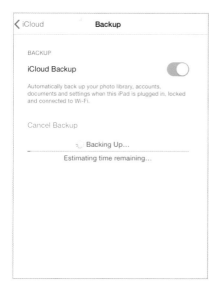

04 You will see an option called 'iCloud Backup'. Ensure that the slider is moved to 'On'.To manage your Storage, head back to the iCloud options and tap 'Storage' and you'll be able to moderate your settings.

05 You will be presented with a message saying that your iPad will no longer sync to iTunes when connected to your computer, just tap 'OK' and wait for a minute while the Backup feature is activated.

06 Your iPad will now back up when connected to a power source and a Wi-Fi network, but you can perform the backup whenever you want by accessing Settings>iCloud and tapping 'Backup Now'.

Set up a Wi-Fi connection

To really make the most of your iPad, you'll want to connect to Wi-Fi and get online. Here's how to do it...

Internet access turns your iPad from an impressive piece of expensive kit into something that opens up worlds. This in part is due to the App Store, a virtual store that gives you access to literally thousands of different applications.

Your iPad is a portal to a host of fantastic services, but first you need to give it access to the internet – only then do your options become plentiful. Follow our simple instructions in this easy-to-follow tutorial and unleash the potential of Apple's powerful device.

Settings Switch on Wi-Fi on your iPad

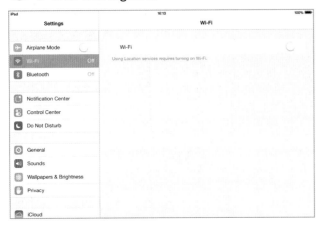

01 You'll find the Setting icon on the main screen, it's silver with cogs in it.

02 After entering Settings, tap on 'Wi-Fi' and then turn it on by sliding the button.

03 Your iPad will now look for available connection points. Tap on your desired connection.

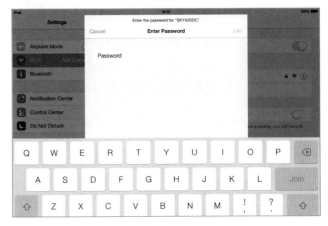

04 Fill out your connection's password details then tap Join and you're done.

Connect to a Bluetooth device

Manage your iPad's Bluetooth connections to other devices easily in just a few simple steps

If you've ever wanted to hook up a wireless speaker, keyboard or even remote control to your iPad, it's probably connecting via Bluetooth. Bluetooth is an incredibly universal technology that allows different devices to connect to each other wirelessly. Managing Bluetooth connections on your iPad is easy as they're all contained within a single settings menu. What's more, the process for setting and up and disconnecting Bluetooth devices is exactly the same, no matter what you're working with.

Settings Manage your iPad's Bluetooth connections

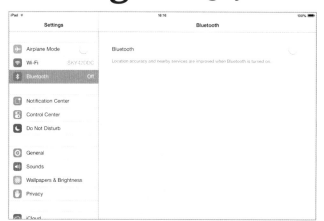

01 In Settings, tap on the 'Bluetooth' tab to view the available devices nearby. Turn your Bluetooth on.

02 Tap on the desired device as it appears on the screen. Your iPad will then start connecting.

03 You may be asked to confirm that a code is correct on each device. Once done this tap Pair.

04 Fill in your details on the keyboard. Once filled in, select Join and you're done.

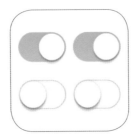

Introducing the Control Centre

Take advantage of your iPad's Control Centre to quickly change settings and access frequently used features

When Control Centre appeared in iOS 7, it was something that users had craved for a long time, but Apple's implementation was arguably even better than we could have hoped for. The elegance with which it works is astounding and a raft of shortcuts and features are available to you with one swipe and a tap.

A lot is happening in a very small space on the iPad and it is surprising that it does not take up more screen real estate, but even this works because you do not have to move your finger much at all to access what you need. Within the pop-up panel you have access to music controls, the Clock app, the camera, AirDrop, AirPlay plus volume and brightness bars. Add to this icons for Airplane mode, Wi-Fi, Bluetooth, Do Not Disturb and screen lock and you can start to see just how effective it can be.

It takes no time to learn and once you start using it, you will wonder how you managed before it arrived, and it will save you so much time if you use your iPad a lot. Now let's explore the Control Centre.

"Once you start using it, you will wonder how you managed before it arrived"

Control Centre Understand the Control Centre

01 Your home screen looks normal until you start to move your finger upwards from below the screen. The Control Centre will start to appear no matter how you swipe up and will take up the bottom proportion of the screen. Notice the semi-transparency behind the panel.

02 The five icons in the middle of the panel will be used the most and as you tap each one text indicators will appear above them. Use these icons to manage Airplane mode, Wi-Fi, Bluetooth, Do Not Disturb and the screen rotation lock. Tap to turn on and off.

Perfect music management
You can play or pause currently playing music and also navigate between tracks using the arrow icons. The volume slider below the icons is particularly useful for music and any other sound-related task that is currently in use

Setting it up
If you have need to limit the use of the Control Centre when using other apps or when the screen is locked you can do so with these settings. Chances are, however, that you likely to not want to do this

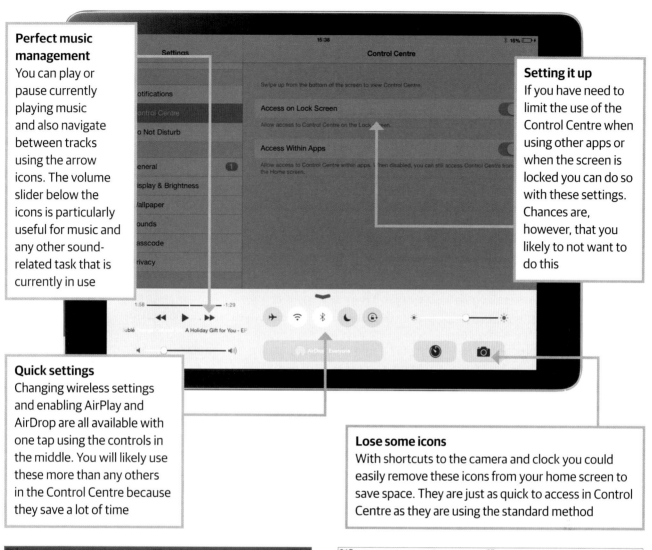

Quick settings
Changing wireless settings and enabling AirPlay and AirDrop are all available with one tap using the controls in the middle. You will likely use these more than any others in the Control Centre because they save a lot of time

Lose some icons
With shortcuts to the camera and clock you could easily remove these icons from your home screen to save space. They are just as quick to access in Control Centre as they are using the standard method

03 To the left you will see icons that can manage music navigation and volume. Simply use the slider for volume and the icons to pause, play and jump between tracks. Over to the right you will find icons to access the camera and clock plus a brightness control.

04 Go to Settings>Control Centre and you will be given two options. The first lets you choose whether to allow access to the Control Centre from the lock screen and the second does the same when you are using a different app. We would advise to turn both on.

Set a passcode lock on your iPad

Protect your iPad from prying eyes and set a passcode that will ensure only you have access to everything

You may store a lot of data on your tablet. Whether it's log-in details for your online accounts, private messages, or documents. If someone could gain access to your iPad, there may be a lot on there that you don't want them to see. Thankfully, Apple's iOS has a very simple way for you to keep your device secure.

Setting a passcode ensures that there is at least some level of protection. Working just like a PIN, you can set a passcode that only you know, and every time you turn your iPad on or unlock it, you'll have to enter this code before gaining access to your iPad.

There are a range of settings that will easily allow you to personalise

your security to the level that you desire. From selecting the option to use a more complex password to erasing all your data upon a number of incorrect entries. No longer will you need to worry about your iPad's data falling into the wrong hands, or jovial friends updating your Facebook status to something untoward.

Settings Turn on Passcode Lock

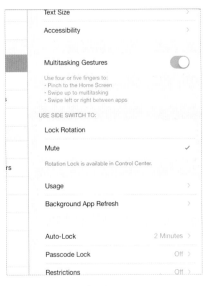

01 From the home screen, you need to select the Settings icon, and then tap on 'General'. You'll find the 'Passcode Lock' option around halfway down. Tap on this to bring up some more specific settings.

02 Within the 'Passcode Lock' setting, you will see this display of options. Currently, there is no passcode set up on this iPad. In order to change this, tap the 'Turn Passcode On' option found at the top.

03 You will be asked to enter a four-digit passcode. Make sure to choose something you'll remember, but nothing too obvious that people will easily guess. Re-enter the code to confirm when asked.

Make a change
If you keep forgetting your passcode, or you think someone else might know it, you can change it anytime by selecting this option

Turn it off
Once you've set a passcode, if you find it a chore to repeatedly keep entering your four digits, you can choose to turn the passcode off

How often?
You can determine how often you need to enter your passcode. If you tire of constantly entering the code, set the length to longer. However, if you wish to keep your phone safe every time you lock it, set it to 'Immediately'

Too simple
Having 'Simple Passcode' set to on means you can set a four-digit passcode. Move the slider to 'Off' and you can enter a longer, more complex passcode for added security

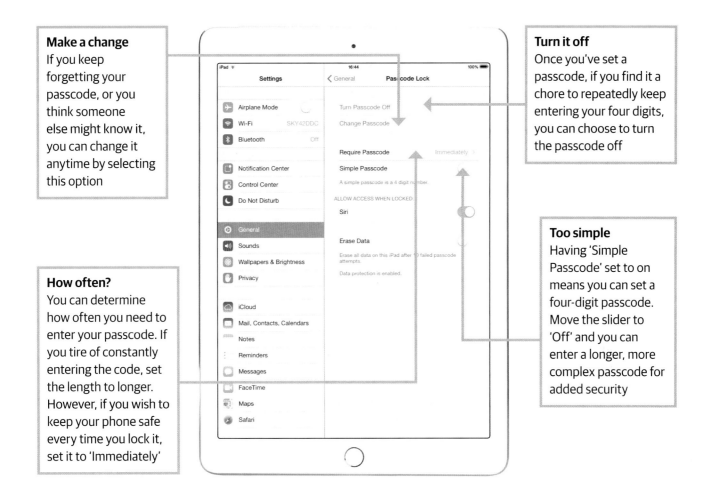

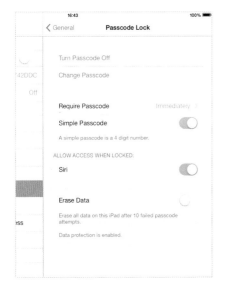

04 Once you have set your passcode, you will notice that a number of extra options are now available on the iPad's screen. You can turn the passcode off, or change the passcode at this point if you so wish.

05 By tapping on the 'Require Passcode' option, you can determine how long after you lock your phone that you need to enter the passcode. Shorter periods of time are safer.

06 If you are not happy with just a four-digit passcode, move the slider on the 'Simple Passcode' option to off. You can then set a longer passcode made up of letters, numbers and special characters.

Control your privacy settings

Keep control of your privacy by monitoring what actions your iPad's apps can and cannot perform

In today's age of digital information, personal details are moved around at a moment's notice. Think about it: your iPad contains a gamut of personal information. How many addresses do you have on your tablet? Do you use your iPad for personal banking? In general terms, you should always be sure to set up the Find My iPhone app, which is supplied by Apple for free and knows what to do if your iPad is lost or stolen.

Thanks to new features introduced recently by Apple, there are other ways to control the privacy of your data. They now allow users to control which apps have access to what kind of data on their tablets, giving you a new level of safety, and peace of mind for all those times when you are not exactly sure whether an app is using information or not. It allows you to secure your device to the level that settles your state of mind. If you don't want any of your private data shared, then you don't have to.

Settings Secure your iPad's privacy

01 The Privacy settings can be found in Settings. They include all the settings you may want to change, such as: Location Services, Contacts, Calendars, Reminders, Photos, Bluetooth Sharing, Twitter and Facebook.

02 Navigating to each of the sections gives you a suitable list of apps that have requested access to various apps on your device. You can enable or disable access via the toggle option located to the right.

03 When you enter this area, you will be told which apps have requested your location. More than that, however, you will also be able to see which app has used location services recently; a good way to monitor activity.

Privacy section
All of the issues relating to privacy on the iPad are stored within this section, which is accessible from your main Settings screen

Your location
When an app has recently looked up your location, an arrow will show up next to its name. Grey arrows denote that an app has looked up your location in the last 24 hours

System apps
System apps like Camera, Maps and Siri will all need to know your location to function properly. These apps can be trusted, so don't worry about switching them on

System services
The System Service area contains options like compass calibration, time zone settings and location-based iAds. None of these are vital, unless you regularly use compass-based directions

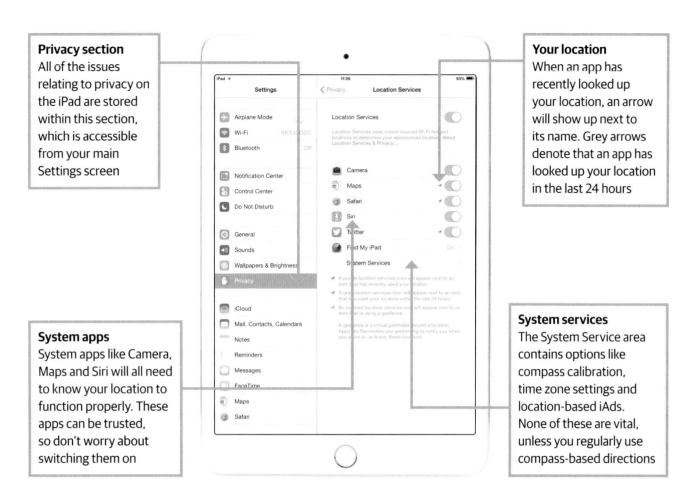

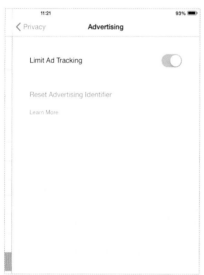

04 In Location Services, you will find that you can enable or disable location services for System Services such as Diagnostics & Usage, Compass Calibration and much more, as shown here.

05 Apps that want to share information via your Bluetooth will appear here. These apps can then share data even when you are not using them, so be careful to monitor this section every now and then.

06 At the bottom of the main Privacy page is a section called Advertising. The new advertising identifier can be used to give you more control over advertisers' ability to use tracking methods on your iPad.

Find a misplaced iPad or iPhone

Keep all of your devices safe at any time and take action to render them impossible to use if they are stolen

Find My iPhone is an app that can be used on any iPad and, despite the name, it has been tweaked to take full advantage of the bigger iPad screen. With this app you can quickly find any iPhone or iPad that signs in using the same Apple ID as your iPad and which is currently connected to the internet. Location Services is used to pinpoint its exact

location at which point you can take different actions remotely. Lost mode will lock the device completely and let you send a personalised message to the device lock screen, you can erase the device with a couple of taps or you can continually play a loud sound. All of this is very useful, but you should at the very least already have a passcode set up

on your device to stop others seeing your data. If your device is powered down or in an area where data coverage is not available, you will not be able to track it, but when turned on Find My iPhone should prove to be useful again. It can make all of the difference between finding your precious device and losing it forever, it is vital to understand how it works.

Find My iPhone Find devices from home

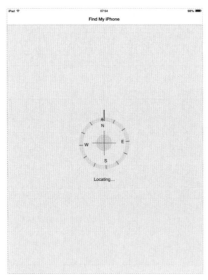

01 Find and install Find My iPhone on the App Store and when opened, you will be prompted to sign in with your Apple ID. Do this with each device your family owns that uses the same Apple ID.

02 The iPad will start searching for devices that are connected to the internet. Initially, this could take a bit of time, but in future searches they should appear very quickly within the main interface.

03 As if by magic, your devices will appear on a real-time map within Find My iPhone. As the devices move, you will see this reflected on the map so you always know exactly where they are.

Find a misplaced iPad or iPhone

Every device covered
All of your Apple devices should be set up with the Find My iPhone app first thing just in case any of them gets lost or is ever stolen

Time to travel
Tapping this icon will immediately open Apple Maps with a route pre-planned for you to travel to where the device currently is

A perfectly tracked phone
Each device will be shown on the map in its exact location any time it is connected. It is a highly accurate and useful solution

Erase a device
If the iPhone or iPad is stolen, you can put it into lost mode or erase it immediately. This will stop whoever has it from using it

04 Tap on any device and a new menu will appear at the bottom of the screen. The name of the device will appear on screen and you'll be able to tap the car icon to receive directions to travel to its location.

05 When you tap 'My Devices' at the top left-hand side of the screen, you will be able to see, and then select, all of your devices in one list. It also shows any devices that have not been connected.

06 If your device has been stolen or you are concerned, you can put it in lost mode remotely or erase it immediately to stop others seeing your personal information. It takes a couple of taps.

Change your iPad's wallpaper

Find out how to quickly customise the background of your iPad's home and lock screens

The iPad enables users the ability to change the background of the home screen as well as the lock screen. This may seem like a trivial addition to the software set but for Apple it's pretty big. It is a company that deals in absolutes and employs a closed system to prevent people making the iOS look bad.

Making changes to the system is very simple; it works in a very similar way to the iPhone, only you can see much more of the action path that you take to get to a change in settings. This makes the system clearer, more memorable and much easier to use. Proficiency at this simple task should give you the courage to explore the

settings further to get even more use from your iPad and make improvements to the way it works for you. Whether it's an image from the iPad's supplied Wallpaper set or a photo from your album, following this step-by-step tutorial will instantly customise your iPad and have it looking the way you want it to.

Settings Change wallpaper

01 Load the Settings and head to 'Wallpaper' on the left hand list. To change your background, simply tap on the pictures beneath 'Choose a New Wallpaper' in the right-hand column of the screen.

02 You now have several options from which to get a suitable picture, do you want your own images or a supplied one? Choose the album that you wish to pick from. Tap on that album to then bring up the contents.

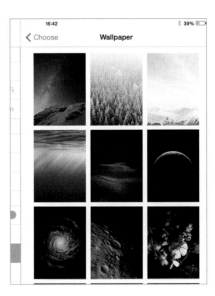

03 Once in the album of your choice, browse the images on offer to make your final selection and then simply tap on that picture. You'll then be taken directly to a preview screen to see your selected image in full.

Simplicity
Apple always makes interfaces easy to use. There's no mass of dialogue and only really a couple of major options here, so it is easy to make changes

Move around
While positioning your picture you will be able to see just how responsive the iPad touch screen is. It's a testament to hardware and software unity

Kill it
Apple also makes it easy for you to change your mind and go back to the last action. In this case just hit the Cancel button

Great resolution
The iPad screen has a fantastic 2048 x 1536 display at 264 pixels per inch (ppi) resolution, so having a cool image on your home and lock screen is a must

04 Use a pinch, reverse pinch and swipe to position the image and then pick from the options at the bottom of the screen: you can pick 'Set Lock Screen', 'Set Home Screen', 'Set Both', or cancel everything.

05 Once you have tapped an option you'll be taken back to the home screen where you can see your changes. Use the Sleep button if you wish to view the lock screen, and obviously you can change it again at any time.

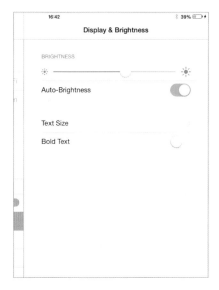

06 Back in iOS 7, adjusting the brightness was under the same option as Wallpaper, however, in iOS 8 you need to head to the 'Display Brightness' tab. Here you can adjust the brightness if you deem it necessary.

Get to grips with multitasking

Multitasking is extremely easy to use in iOS 8 and there are many useful features available using just a swipe and a tap

Multitasking has been available on the iPad since it first arrived on the shelves, but recent changes mean that it is easier to use than ever before. Gone is the small strip of icons at the bottom of the screen when you double-tap the home button and in its place is a full screen display that lets you move between apps with ease.

Each app is obviously presented thanks to the large screenshots which show the last position the app reached and the app icons directly below each shot to clarify. You can swipe up on the main panel to close an app fully or tap it to open it immediately. It sounds like a small change, but for a feature that you will likely use often it really does make the process much quicker

and efficient when used often. In addition, with iOS 8 you can now view your most recently used contacts at the top of the screen. You can contact them simply by tapping on their picture (or their initials if you haven't programmed a picture for their profile). It really is a great way to get around your iPad.

> **"It really does make the process much quicker and efficient when used often"**

Multitasking Understand the multitasking feature

01 Double-tap the home button no matter what you are doing on your iPad and a series of horizontal panels will appear on the screen. Below each you will see an icon which is designed to show what app you are looking at. The panels show where the app froze.

02 To switch between apps, simply scroll your finger left and all of the recently used and open apps will be shown. You can now tap either the app icon or the main panel to jump straight to that app. It should start up in the exact position you left it in.

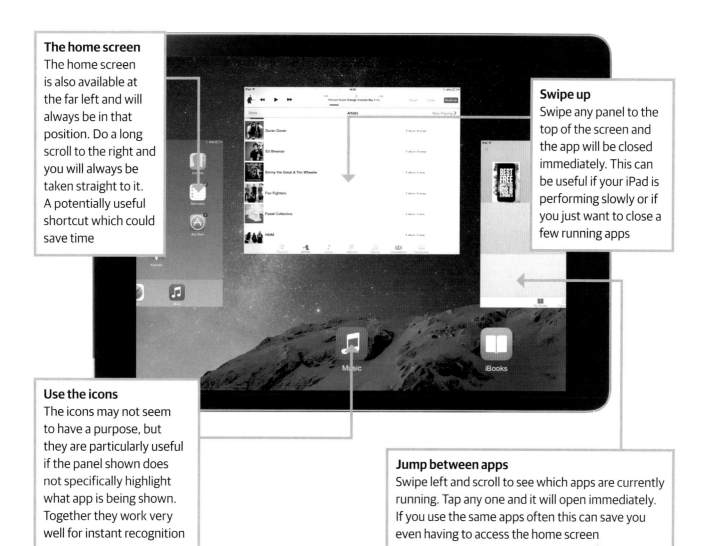

The home screen
The home screen is also available at the far left and will always be in that position. Do a long scroll to the right and you will always be taken straight to it. A potentially useful shortcut which could save time

Swipe up
Swipe any panel to the top of the screen and the app will be closed immediately. This can be useful if your iPad is performing slowly or if you just want to close a few running apps

Use the icons
The icons may not seem to have a purpose, but they are particularly useful if the panel shown does not specifically highlight what app is being shown. Together they work very well for instant recognition

Jump between apps
Swipe left and scroll to see which apps are currently running. Tap any one and it will open immediately. If you use the same apps often this can save you even having to access the home screen

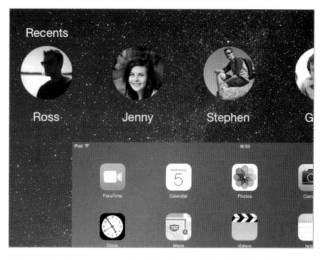

03 If you want to close an app hold your finger on a panel and then slide it to the top of the screen. The panel will disappear and the app to the right will slide over to take its place. The sheer size of the panels makes closing apps very simple.

04 There is one final feature of the Multitasking feature that was brand-new with iOS 8, the ability to view your most recent contacts at the top. You'll be able to access your contacts by tapping their picture, or their initials.

Access email on your iPad

Set up your email accounts on your iPad for even better usage than your iPhone can provide

In today's digital age, using email is one of the most essential ways of being able to stay in touch with friends and family wherever they are in the world, as well as being a pretty vital tool in the business world. While both the iPhone and iPod touch are perfectly capable of displaying email, the iPad is just so much better due to its larger size, making it a much superior option, especially with the additions Apple have made over the last few iOS updates. The virtual

keyboard makes it far easier and quicker to type on (especially when you need to write longer emails), in turn making it far more practical to use day in day out.

This step-by-step tutorial will not only show you how to set up a new or existing email account for use on the iPad and beyond, but will also

take you through the fundamentals of reading and sending email. Once set up you'll be able to use existing accounts at will, quickly reply and forward mail that you receive, and, most importantly, ensure that you stay in touch with friends and loved ones. Basically, you will never look at your iPad in the same way again.

"You will never look at your iPad in the same way again"

Mail Set up an email account on your iPad

01 In order to set up an email account you will need to first enter the Settings app of your iPad. Look at the icons on the home page of your iPad until you find one with a large, grey cog. Tap on it to continue to the Settings menu. It may be at the bottom of the screen.

02 Upon entering Settings you'll find a row of different icons down the left-hand side of the screen. Look for and select 'Mail, Contacts, Calendars' in order to continue. Now look on the right-hand side of the screen and tap on 'Add Account'.

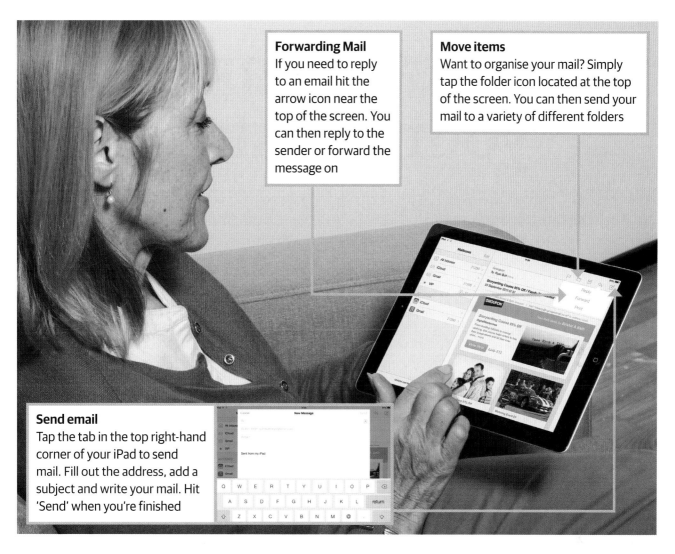

Forwarding Mail
If you need to reply to an email hit the arrow icon near the top of the screen. You can then reply to the sender or forward the message on

Move items
Want to organise your mail? Simply tap the folder icon located at the top of the screen. You can then send your mail to a variety of different folders

Send email
Tap the tab in the top right-hand corner of your iPad to send mail. Fill out the address, add a subject and write your mail. Hit 'Send' when you're finished

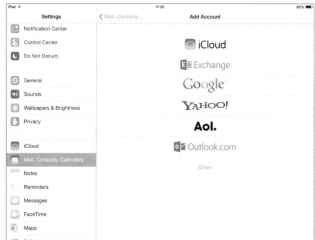

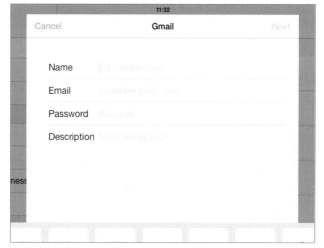

03 You'll now be presented with seven account options. They are iCloud, Microsoft Exchange, Google Mail, Yahoo! Mail, AOL, Microsoft Hotmail and Other. Whether you want to create a new account or add an existing one, the process is as follows...

04 After choosing your account you'll be presented with the following screen. All you need to do here is fill in the relevant information for each section. Once this is done simply tap on 'Next' in the top right-hand corner. Congratulations, you have mail.

Install iTunes on your desktop

Installing iTunes on your Mac or PC will allow you to sync up your music with your device

Since the release of iOS 5, all of Apple's devices, including your iPad, can be used straight out of the box without the need to connect them to your computer via iTunes, as was previously the case.

However, installing the latest copy of iTunes on your computer is still recommended as it allows you to perform a series of useful tasks.

Primarily, through iTunes you can still convert your CD collection and then copy the files to your iPad, but the latest version, 11, fully embraces Apple's iTunes in the iCloud service so that any music you purchase through iTunes – be it on your iPad or Mac – is automatically pushed to all of your devices wirelessly. What's more, through iTunes Match you can also access your entire iTunes library from any device, streaming individual tracks or downloading them for offline listening for a small annual cost (£21.99/$24.99). You can also connect your iPad to your computer via USB and perform essential backup and syncing processes.

In this tutorial we guide you through the process of downloading and installing the latest version.

> **"Through iTunes Match you can access your iTunes library from any device"**

iTunes Installing iTunes on your Mac or PC

01 Launch your preferred browser and head to **www.itunes.com**. The layout of the page changes regularly, but there will be a 'Download iTunes' button somewhere within it (currently, it's located in the top-right of the page).

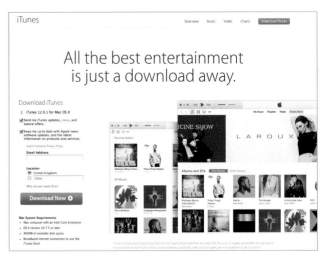

02 Your browser will recognise the type of computer you're on (Windows or Mac) to avoid confusion. You'll see a single 'Download Now' button. Be sure to double-check you're happy with the options to receive emails from Apple.

Automatic detection
All modern browsers transmit what type of computer you are currently using and clever websites can take advantage of that information to only offer you the choices that match those criteria

Privacy Policy
If you're concerned about what Apple might do with the information you give them (namely, your email address, as requested on this page), you can check out its policy by clicking here

Email notifications
By default, these two tick boxes are enabled, which means that you won't be able to download iTunes without typing in your email address first. If you'd rather stay anonymous, untick them

System Requirements
If you're at all uncertain if your computer will be able to run the software, this section displays the necessary system requirements that match the machine you're currently running

03 Once the download is complete, a new window will open up with a iTunes logo inside it. The 'Read Before You Install iTunes' document gives you the minimum requirements without which the program will not function. Double-click 'Install iTunes' to proceed.

04 Once iTunes has been installed, its icon should appear in your Dock or Desktop. If it hasn't, you'll be able to locate it in your Applications or Program Files folder. The first time you double-click on it, you'll have to agree to the licence agreement.

Get to know the iTunes interface

iTunes is no longer just a means to play your music, but gives you instant access to the iTunes store and much more!

The first version of iTunes was released over a decade ago, back on 9 January 2001. Apple had purchased Casady and Greene's SoundJam MP two years previously, realising that it had missed the boat with regards to the CD ripping and burning that was going on at the time. The iPod didn't even exist. Three years later, however, the iTunes Music Store was born, along with Apple's ambitions as an online entertainment retailer.

It's only recently that you can actually use your iPad without first installing iTunes on your computer, and since the release of iOS 5 you can activate your device and get all the latest system updates without the need to manually connect it to. However, there is a lot more to iTunes than allowing iPad

functionality, not least the ability to convert your CD collection to MP3 format and copy the tracks to your device, browse for all the latest entertainment and apps at the iTunes and App Stores and enjoy the many new features that iCloud provides. Here we show you the basics of its functionality.

"It's only recently that you can actually use your iPad without installing iTunes"

iTunes Getting to know the software

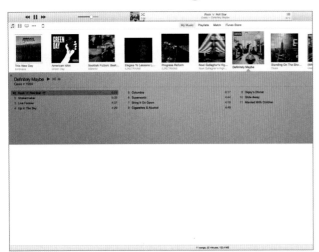

01 Your media is broken down by type – ie music, books and videos etc – all of which you can acquire from the iTunes Store. To sort between these, simply click on the current category button and select a new one from the drop-down list.

02 To access Apple's online media store, move your cursor up to the right-hand side of the top menu bar and click on 'iTunes Store'. The front page is geared towards entertainment, showing you the latest and most popular songs and albums, films and TV shows.

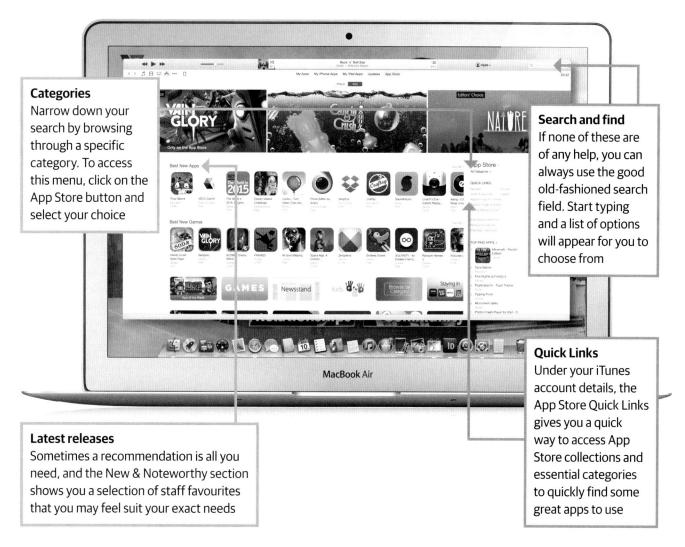

Categories
Narrow down your search by browsing through a specific category. To access this menu, click on the App Store button and select your choice

Search and find
If none of these are of any help, you can always use the good old-fashioned search field. Start typing and a list of options will appear for you to choose from

Quick Links
Under your iTunes account details, the App Store Quick Links gives you a quick way to access App Store collections and essential categories to quickly find some great apps to use

Latest releases
Sometimes a recommendation is all you need, and the New & Noteworthy section shows you a selection of staff favourites that you may feel suit your exact needs

03 To get to the App Store and start browsing for applications for your iPad, head back to the row of buttons just above the main content window in iTunes and click on 'App Store'. Once there, you'll see two buttons centred immediately below the menu bar. Click on 'iPad'.

04 After activating your iPad, it'll appear on the right-hand side of the top menu bar in the main library view. Click on its to you'll gain access to your device's sync settings. You can add everything automatically or select which media and apps to add.

Sync your music from iTunes

Discover just how easy it is to sync your music collection from a computer to your iPad

Playing music on your iPad is the closest thing you'll get to using the full desktop version of iTunes on the go. Getting music onto your iPad is a simple process through iTunes. It's possible to sync tracks, albums or your entire music library. iTunes remembers your settings, so whenever your iPad is plugged into the computer it automatically syncs any new music tracks to the device. By spending just a few minutes setting up your music sync options and you won't have to manually add tracks ever again.

iTunes Get your music on your iPad

01 Make sure you have music in you iTunes, rip music from CDs or buy tracks from the iTunes store.

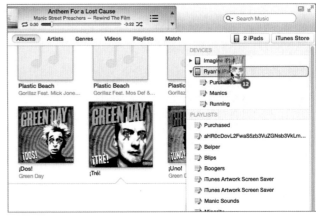

02 Connect your iPad, then you can manually drag songs or click on 'Music' in its settings.

03 Once you're happy with the selection, click the 'Apply/Sync' button at the bottom of the screen.

04 Once the syncing process has been completed, you can listen to your music on your iPad.

Transfer movies using iTunes

We explain how easy it is to copy movies from your desktop computer to an iPad

Wherever you are, watching movies on your iPad is a marvel. It gets even better if the movie has been purchased or rented through the iTunes Store, as the iPad will display detailed information about the film and enable users to skip directly to a particular chapter with just one tap of the finger. Making the film waching experience that much better on your iPad.

In this tutorial we shall cover how you can simply sync your movies to your iPad to watch on the go.

iTunes Sync your movies to your iPad

01 Purchase movies from the iTunes store, or import files, .MOV/.MP4 are compatible.

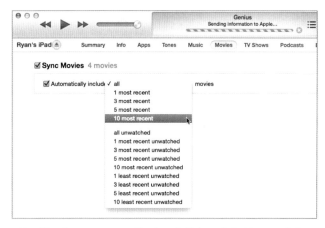

02 Connect your iPad and click on it in iTunes. Select the Films tab then check the Sync Films button.

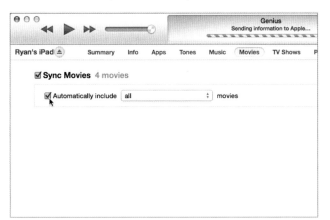

03 Select the films that you wish to sync, Once you're happy, click the 'Apply/Sync' button.

04 Once the films have copied you can watch them from the Videos app.

Sync your books through iTunes

Find out how to sync books with your iPad, and where to download the latest titles

Before the iPad was even announced, media pundits were declaring it to be the saviour of print media. Both the iPad and iPad mini's display makes reading text a joy, particularly when combined with the Retina display on the iPad. eBooks can either be synced from a desktop computer or purchased directly from Apple's iBooks app – and if downloading books to your computer, you can also use the 'Automatic Downloads' iCloud feature (go to Settings>Store and activate the options).

iTunes Sync eBooks to your iPad

01 Go to the iTunes Store and click on the 'Books' tab. Purchases will be added to your 'Books' library.

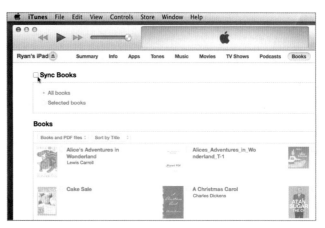

02 Plug your iPad into the computer. After syncing, click on the 'iPad' button, then 'Books.

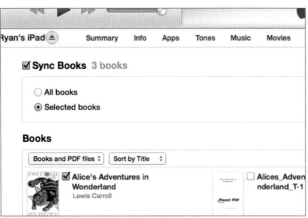

03 From here you can choose what to sync. Then click the 'Apply/Sync' button.

04 You can also download books from the app by tapping 'Store' in the top corner.

Put photos on your iPad

In this guide we'll show you how easy it is to sync photographs from your Mac/PC to an iPad

The iPad is the perfect device for displaying photos. It's by far the best way to show off your latest snaps as the device can be passed from person to person.

There are a handful of ways to get your favourite photos onto your iPad. They can be synced from a Mac/PC, emailed or imported from an SD card and, thanks to the

iCloud's Photo Stream feature, even beamed wirelessly to your device automatically. In this tutorial we explain how to transfer images from your computer using iTunes.

iTunes Get your photos on your iPad via iTunes

01 Open iTunes, then plug the iPad and sync. Once done, click on your 'iPad' button in iTunes.

02 At the top of the screen are various buttons for syncing media – click on the 'Photos' button.

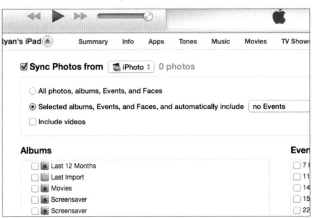

03 Click on the check box and choose a folder from your computer. When correct, click OK.

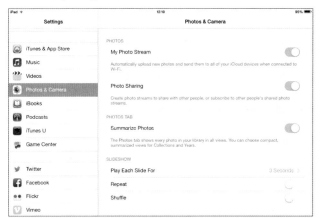

04 Go to Settings>Photos to turn Photo Stream on to automatically get photos from your Mac/PC.

Getting started

All the basics are covered here to get you in control of your iPad

"Make the most of the
iPad's built-in apps"

59

Move icons and use folders

Keep your iPad menu tidy by organising the menus by creating folders and moving icons

Whenever a new app is installed, it just gets added to the end of the existing list, or if there's a gap anywhere, it can appear there. This is fine when you only have a handful of apps, but after a couple of months with your iPad, the screens start to fill up and it all looks disorganised and messy; a general hubbub of apps in no real sensible order. Fortunately it can all be organised into areas of

similar functions, such as games on one page, utilities on another and reference apps on a page as well.

You can reorganise your iPad screens using iTunes, where it is easy to create extra screens, even if the current ones are full, but it's also possible to move icons around directly on the iPad itself. Also,

you can create as many folders as you like and bundle apps together in order to make your display very neat and tidy.

The final benefits are that unwanted apps can be deleted and must-have apps can be added to the Dock bar at the bottom of every screen.

"You can bundle apps together to make your display very neat and tidy"

Home screen Keep your iPad organised

01 Turn your iPad on so that you are looking at your home screen. If you have lots of apps then the icons for them will be spread over subsequent screens. To arrange them together tap and hold an app you want to move until all the apps start to wiggle.

02 Still holding down on the app, drag your finger to the edge of the screen you want to move to. The apps will then scroll sideways to pull the next screen into view. Now move your finger over the place where you want the app to go and then let go of it.

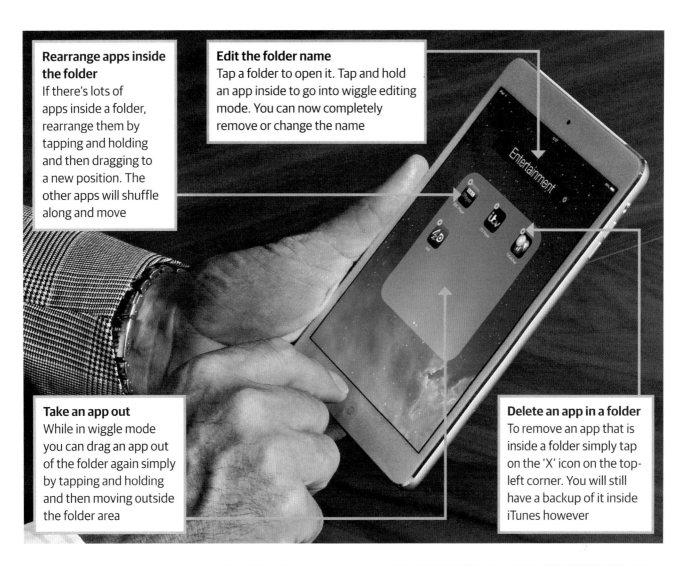

Rearrange apps inside the folder
If there's lots of apps inside a folder, rearrange them by tapping and holding and then dragging to a new position. The other apps will shuffle along and move

Edit the folder name
Tap a folder to open it. Tap and hold an app inside to go into wiggle editing mode. You can now completely remove or change the name

Take an app out
While in wiggle mode you can drag an app out of the folder again simply by tapping and holding and then moving outside the folder area

Delete an app in a folder
To remove an app that is inside a folder simply tap on the 'X' icon on the top-left corner. You will still have a backup of it inside iTunes however

03 Press the Home button to return your iPad to normal. To create folders, drop an app over the top of one you want it to appear in a folder with. A folder is then instantly created with a name that reflects the type of apps, if they are fairly similar.

04 If the folder name isn't to your liking, simply tap on the 'X' icon to delete it and tap in the text field to enter your own. When complete, press the Home button twice to exit. To add more apps to the same folder, simply drag and drop them into it.

Discover the features of Safari

Safari didn't go forgotten in the iOS 7 make over, here we take you through the features you shouldn't miss out on

Safari has long been considered one of the best mobile browsers. It mixes a simple user interface with great functionality and plenty of additional features to keep everybody happy. Apple isn't a company to stand still, and when iOS 7 came out in 2013, Safari was given a tidy new facelift.

The main features involve the continued move to cloud computing and the aim of seamlessly syncing between various devices. To do so,

Apple has introduced iCloud Tabs, which means you'll never need to email a link to yourself. Flicking through a webpage on your iPhone at work, but you want to view it on your iPad at home? iCloud Tabs ensures that a webpage is instantly loaded in any browser linked with your iCloud account.

iCloud Tabs is just the tip of the iceberg. There's also the Offline Reading List function that lets you view webpages regardless of your internet connection, while Facebook and Twitter integration also makes life easier. Here we take you through these features in a bit more detail, as well as a few more to boot.

"Safari mixes a simple user interface with great functionality and additional features"

Safari Explore Safari's best features

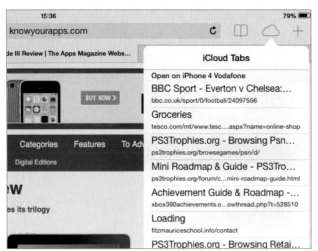

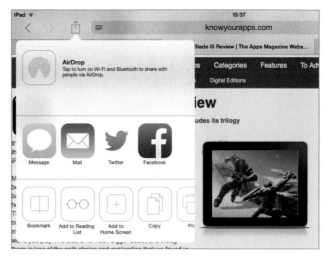

01 Ensure that all your devices are running with the same iCloud account by using the Settings app on any device. Safari will also need to be activated under the services that are set to sync through your account. iCloud Tabs will appear under the cloud symbol in your browser.

02 When you save an article for later reading, it's saved to your device so you can view it even if you're offline. Find an article, hit the Share icon (the arrow and box next to the left of the address bar) and tap the 'Add to Reading List' option to get started.

Reading List
On the surface, your Reading List service looks exactly as it did previously. As we've explained, there's a lot more to it now. Hit this tab and you'll be able to view anything you save regardless of your internet connection speed

Social networks
Safari continues to support Facebook and Twitter. Here you have the ability to share articles or webpages to your News Feed by tapping the share icon and then choosing the Twitter or Facebook options

Extra tabs
This may not be something that you will pick up on straight away, but Safari now enables you to have more tabs open than ever before. In fact, on your iPad, you'll be able to have 24 tabs open simultaneously

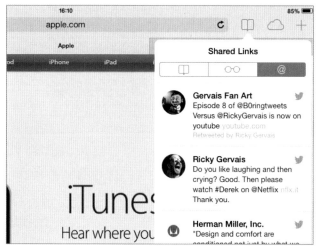

03 As well as being able to tweet straight from Safari by tapping on the share icon and choosing Twitter, you can also instantly read all of the latest tweets of the people you following by tapping the book icon and then selecting the '@' tab in the window that appears.

04 iOS 8 continues to make it easy to communicate information through your social networks straight from Safari. You can share webpages in a matter of seconds; simply hit the Share button and then the Facebook icon to post with a message.

De-clutter the web with Safari Reader

Thanks to a new Safari feature, you can read fresh web content devoid of intrusive ads and page furniture

Browsing web pages through Safari on your iPad is a pleasurable experience thanks to its intuitive interface and useful features designed to make surfing the internet as effortless and enjoyable as possible.

The app got even better too, thanks to the iOS 5 update that introduced additional elements such as tabbed pages and a Reading List. But perhaps one of the best elements of Safari's arsenal of cool features is Reader.

This feature enables you to read and enjoy web articles free from clutter such as intrusive ad banners and links. If you have accessed a page that can benefit from the Safari Reader function then a list icon will be visible next to the address bar. Tap on it and the page will undergo an instant transformation into a cleaner, easier-to-read format. This is particularly useful for reading longer articles when you don't want to be distracted. It's quick and easy to use, and when you've read the article you can return the page to its original state by tapping the list icon again.

Safari How to use Reader

01 Safari Reader is a service that came as part of iOS 5, so connect your device to your computer through iTunes and make sure that your installed iOS version is 5 or higher. After this the service should be available to you.

02 Launch your Safari app to access the internet and then start browsing. As you access various pages, keep an eye on the address bar for the tell-tale list icon that signifies that the page you are on is compatible.

03 If a page is compatible with Reader, a small list icon will be visible to the left of the URL bar. Tap on this icon to transform the page into a clear, easy-to-read format, and rid the page of banners and ads.

De-clutter the web with Safari Reader

Sharing stories
You can share stories from Safari Reader as you would through the normal Safari view – just tap on the sharing icon

Reader icon
When a page is compatible with Reader, look out for the list icon next to the address bar and tap it to strip the page of all its clutter and ads

Reading List
To store the article safely, without having to create a new bookmark, tap on the sharing icon and choose 'Add to Reading List'

A cleaner look
Pages that are being viewed through Reader feature only the main text, with all side panels and ads stripped out for a fresher, uncluttered look

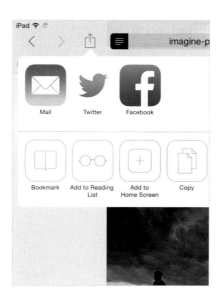

04 By tapping on the sharing icon in the top-left corner of the interface, you can open up a menu of different ways in which you can share the story with other people. These ways include email and social media.

05 If you don't have time to read your current article in its entirety, then you can add it to your 'Reading List' to read at a later time. Tap on the sharing icon in the top-left corner and choose 'Add to Reading List'.

06 When you've read the article and are finished with it, tap on the 'Reader' icon again and your page will return to its previous state. This way you'll be able to continue browsing the internet as normal.

Explore the Mail app

Learn how to send and receive emails through your iPad's built in iOS 8 Mail app, and see what features it has to offer

One of the main things people do with the tablets is send and read emails. The large touch screen makes it a beautifully simple way to view your mail, and with messages displaying photos inside the message itself, it's so much more engaging.

In iOS 8, Apple hasn't changed the formula of Mail too much – it still displays your messages in much the same way, the most notable difference you'll find is when you swipe across messages in your inbox you will get various options for handling them, such as Flag and Archive.

You can pull down from the top of the screen to refresh the list, and add images to messages simply by tapping anywhere within a new email and choosing the 'Insert Photo or Video' option. What's also handy is the way you can mark senders as VIPs. This great feature marks incoming messages from VIPs with a star and separates them into their own tidy inbox so that you can find them quickly and easily when needed.

Mail Use the best features of Mail

01 If you swipe down on your inbox, you can pull the list of current emails down – this gesture prompts the Mail app to check the server for new messages and will display any new ones clearly for you to view.

02 To create a new email, simply tap on the pad and pen icon in the top-right corner of the inbox screen. To add a recipient simply tap on the 'To:' box and type in their credentials. Add a subject and type in your message.

03 It's very easy to add an image to an email; simply double-tap in the main area and then choose 'Insert Photo or Video'. Select your image from that pop-up menu and hit 'Add'. It will insert itself into the email.

Pull to refresh
It might seem like a small thing, but Pull to Refresh really will change the way you read emails on your iPad, with a simple, time-saving gesture

Extra signatures
Until recently, you were limited to only one signature that was added to every account. In iOS 8 you can add one signature for each account – perfect for if you use your iPad for both work and personal emails

Starry eyes
VIPs are sorted from other email senders with a star next to the emails they send. Unread messages have blue stars, while read messages appear like this

Photo opportunity
Whereas sending photos used to require you to use the Photos app, you can now add photos within Mail itself, which is very useful

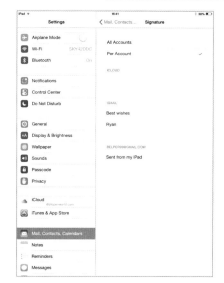

04
You can also add multiple signatures to your accounts in the Settings app, by going to 'Mail, Contacts & Calendars', choosing 'Signature' and then 'Per Account', before typing out a signature.

05
To make a contact into a VIP, click their name and then choose 'Add to VIP' from the bottom of the list in the drop-down menu. This means you will be alerted when an email from them arrives in your mailbox.

06
You can customise Notifications for VIP messages in the Notifications section of the Settings app. This way you will always know when your VIPs send you an email, and view it immediately.

Add media to Mail messages

Adding media attachments to emails is no longer a battle; now it's the work of a couple of clicks

It may be hard to believe but it was once quite a hassle to email images and videos to friends from your iPad. In those dark days, you had to adopt an awkward workaround: first open up the Photos app, then select the video or picture you want to send and finally email it from within that app. When you think about it, it was an odd way to go about things; surely you should be sending email attachments from Mail?

Well, ever since iOS 7, things are more like you would expect them to be for an Apple device. You can treat media attachments in the same way as you would in an email application on your computer – by adding them within the body of an email message. With a couple of taps inside your email message, you can open a media browser, add the video or image inside the body of the email, and then send it when you are ready. And while there was once a limitation to the number of videos or images you could send at one time, you can now add as many images as you want straight from within the Mail app.

"Treat media attachments in the same way as you would in on your computer"

Mail Adding photos or video to email

01 To add a photo or video inside the body of an email, open up the Mail app and tap the 'Compose' button to start a new message. Tap inside the empty body of the message to bring up a popover menu. From this menu, choose 'Insert Photo or Video'.

02 You can then choose the video or photo you want to add, either from your Camera Roll or from your Photo Stream. Tap the thumbnail preview of the one you want to add and it will appear in a Preview window. To add it to the email, tap 'Use'.

Inline images
Images or videos that you add appear in the body of the email. You can add more than one image or video to each email

Preview images
You preview images in this window before you commit to adding them to the email message. If you like what you see, tap the 'Use' button. If you tap 'Cancel' you can return to choose another image

Adding more
Add more images by double-tapping on an existing image or video. This brings up the popover menu that will let you insert a photo or video nest to the media you just tapped

Adding an image
You can tap in an empty area of the body of the email to bring up the popover menu. This lets you add images or videos directly into the body of your email

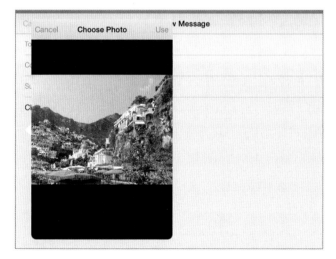

03 The image or video should now appear inside your email message. To add more images or videos to the email, just repeat the processes in steps 1 and 2, tapping inside the email message and then selecting the 'Insert Photo or Video' menu option.

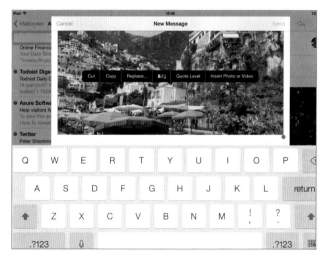

04 If you change your mind, you can delete media from your email message. Tap and hold on the image to delete so it's highlighted and then select 'Cut' from the popover menu. When you've finalised your image selection, tap the 'Send' button to send your email.

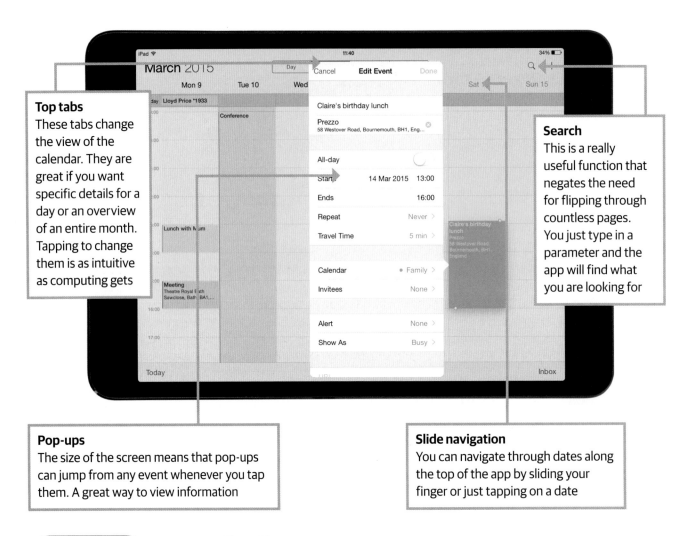

Top tabs
These tabs change the view of the calendar. They are great if you want specific details for a day or an overview of an entire month. Tapping to change them is as intuitive as computing gets

Search
This is a really useful function that negates the need for flipping through countless pages. You just type in a parameter and the app will find what you are looking for

Pop-ups
The size of the screen means that pop-ups can jump from any event whenever you tap them. A great way to view information

Slide navigation
You can navigate through dates along the top of the app by sliding your finger or just tapping on a date

Tuesday 10

Add an event in Calendar

If you find yourself struggling to remember your schedule, make sure you never miss an important event with your iPad

The Calendar app on the iPhone is useful and easy to use, but it gets dwarfed by the sheer scale of the iPad equivalent. Like the Contacts app, Apple has gone with the classic analogue look and made the app look like an old-school, physical calendar. Of course, this digital version has a multitude of advantages over a real one. Firstly, you get the beauty of typeface, rather than scrawled handwriting. Secondly, it's easy to undo mistakes. Thirdly, you can view it in a number of different ways.

Like all the iPad apps, the Calendar app is easy to use. Adding an event is simplicity itself, and the large screen size means that pop-up windows replace the screen shunting right or left as it does on the iPhone. All you need remains in front of you at all times. Once your events are created they can be edited and you can view them in a number of ways as you change orientation or as you dictate on the top tabs of the app.

Calendar Add an event

01 Open the Calendar app and turn the iPad horizontal to see the dual-page layout. Navigate to the day you want and then tap the '+' button in the top right corner. This way you'll create a new event.

02 A small pop-up window will appear in the top-right, and the keyboard will show up too. Tap the field you wish to edit – such as 'Title' – and then name your event by using the keyboard.

03 You can add as much or as little detail as you want, including the location and duration of the event, as well as invitees. You have access to a full keyboard so you can go to town on the detail.

04 You now need to add the start and end date of your event, just to make sure you don't miss it! Tap on the relevant field to see the pop-up change into a new window display.

05 Use the wheels to select the times and dates that you want to use. You can also toggle the 'All-day' button instead if the event that is taking place will take up the entire day.

06 When you have everything in place, you need to tap the 'Add' button located in the top-right corner of the window. Alternatively you can cancel it to return without saving.

07 Tap the 'Alert' field to set reminders for the event. These will help ensure you don't miss an appointment. Alerts pop up on your iPad at the times you set them.

08 There are a number of options, ranging from at the event time to two days before. Tap on your desired option and save your progress by clicking 'Done'.

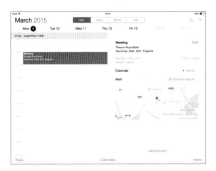

09 Save your event and it will appear on the page. Tap on it to see its details and to make changes. You can erase it by tapping the red 'Delete Event' button below.

Keep perfect time with Clock

We take an in-depth look at your iPad's native Clock app and what it can do for you

The iPad's native Clock app is a versatile little beast that can carry out four simple and incredibly useful tasks. The first option, selectable via the icons at the bottom of the interface, is World Clock and this allows you to track the time in up to 12 locations around the world. Useful for work purposes if you are dealing with overseas clients or for finding the most sociable time to call friends on the other side of the world, you simply tap on one of the '+' slots and pick a location to add.

The next function is Alarm – we'll look at this function in more detail shortly. The other two functions are Stopwatch and Timer. Stopwatch provides a timer that counts down when you tap the Start button, and get lap times by tapping the Lap button to record each checkpoint. Timer offers an accurate countdown from a predetermined time, useful for cooking, or use it to automatically turn off your music if you listen to it on you iPad when getting to sleep. Once you explore this app's functions you'll wonder how you ever managed without it.

Clock Set an alarm

01 Tap on the Alarm icon at the bottom of the interface, and then tap on the '+' icon in the top-right corner of the screen to bring up a new alarm details box. You can add as many alarms as you like throughout the day.

02 Tap on either of the two digit sliders to set them to the time you want your alarm to sound. From this box you can also program repeats – handy if you use the alarm every day. You can repeat as many times as you want.

03 Tap on the Sound menu and you can choose an alarm sound from a wide range of pre-installed options. You can also tap 'Pick a song' to choose from your own Music library. Tap the '+' button next to the song to set it.

Keep perfect time with Clock

Your alarms
The alarms you set will be instantly identifiable on a handy week grid. You can press and hold and drag them to new time slots or change details by tapping 'Edit' in the top-left corner

Adding alarms
Tap on the '+' icon in the top-right corner of the interface to create new alarms. The details box allows you to set the time, repeat the alarm, choose your chime and more

Clock app modes
Tap on the icons at the bottom of the interface to access the four functions of the Clock app, which are World Clock, Alarm, Stopwatch and Timer

Snooze function
If you have the Snooze function enabled in your alarms (by moving the green slider to the On position in the alarm details box) then you can tap to Snooze when the alert pops up

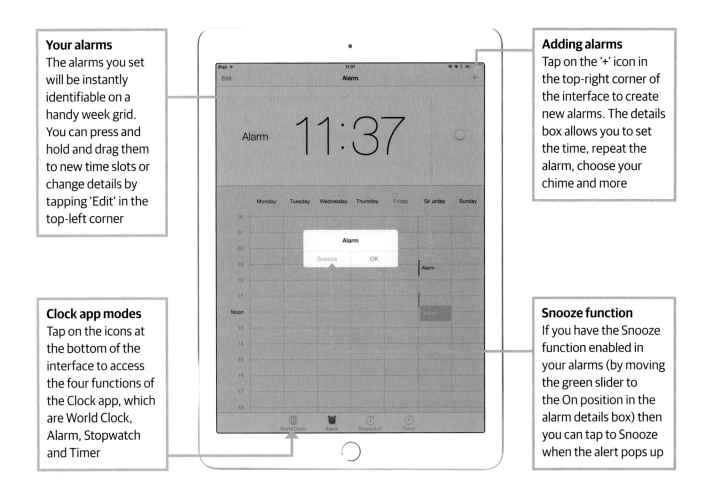

04 Before closing this window, ensure that the 'Snooze' option is enabled to allow you to temporarily disable the alarm when it sounds. When you are finished, tap 'Save' in the top-right corner of the window.

05 You can move an alarm to a different time by pressing and holding on it and dragging it to a new time slot. To edit alarms, tap 'Edit' in the top-left corner and then either delete or edit the details of an alarm.

06 If you have an alarm set that you know you are not going to need, simply move the green slider to the right of the alarm time to the off position rather than deleting it entirely, just in case you want to use it again.

Use Reminders to never miss events

Thanks to Apple's task management app, you have no excuse for forgetting birthdays

We all like to think that our minds operate like super-computers. As such, we utter the words, "Don't worry, I'll remember..." on an all-too regular basis, only to forget whatever it was we said we'd never forget. To help, Apple has created its own task management app, and it's a cracker.

Reminders lets you organise your life into To Do lists, complete with due dates, notes and reminders to ensure that you never forget when something important is pressing.

Simply jot down tasks, record when you need to do them by, then tick each one off as you complete it. Reminders is location-based, so if you need to pick up some groceries from the supermarket, you can be alerted as soon as you pull in to the car park. The app also works with Calendar, Outlook and iCloud, so any changes you make to your Reminders list will update automatically on all them. Here we guide you through the process of setting your own reminders and managing your To Do lists.

Reminders Setting yourself reminders

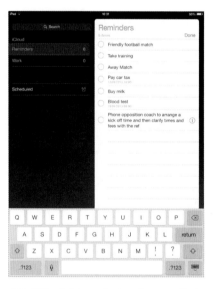

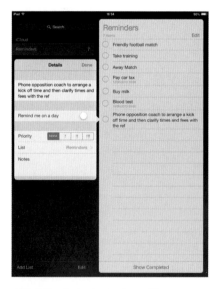

01 When you first open Reminders you can immediately start compiling a To Do list by tapping the 'Add List' button in the bottom-left corner. Use the default keyboard to type your reminder.

02 Add reminders to your To Do list by simply tapping on the newly created list. The lines on the paper will even expand to neatly contain all of your text – just in case you have a complicated task that you need to complete!

03 Select a task and tap on the 'i' icon to view your details. Tap 'Remind me on a day' to 'On', then use the trusty wheels and program it to the date of your choosing when your device should alert you.

Use Reminders to never miss events

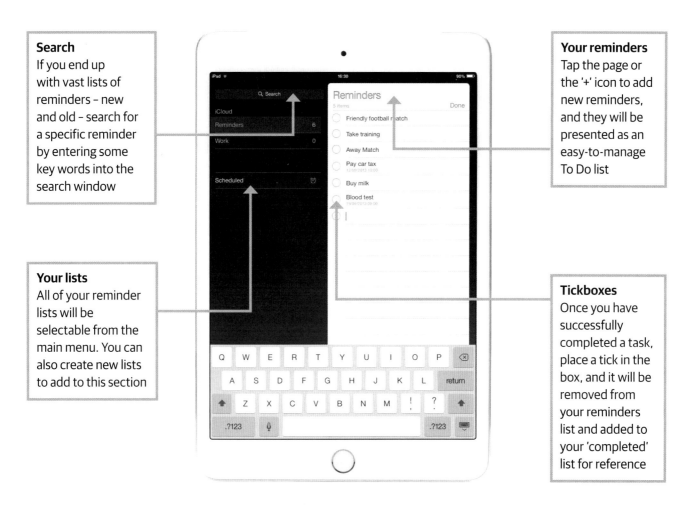

Search
If you end up with vast lists of reminders – new and old – search for a specific reminder by entering some key words into the search window

Your reminders
Tap the page or the '+' icon to add new reminders, and they will be presented as an easy-to-manage To Do list

Your lists
All of your reminder lists will be selectable from the main menu. You can also create new lists to add to this section

Tickboxes
Once you have successfully completed a task, place a tick in the box, and it will be removed from your reminders list and added to your 'completed' list for reference

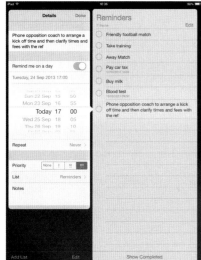

04 You can set various other options, such as the priority, which list it relates to and add notes that relate to each task if you feel you may need more information. Tap 'Done' when you're happy. You can edit at any time.

05 If the item you need reminding of is a frequent occurrence then you can also tap on Repeat and then set yourself a timescale for repeating the reminder, whether it be every day, every week or every month.

06 Whenever a task is completed, tap the box next to it to add a mark. Reminders that have been marked will be added to your Completed list, making you feel good about yourself! They are viewable at any time.

Edit Notification Center settings

Make sure you never miss a thing by setting up your very own personalised Notification Center

Your iPad has always been good at notifying you about updates, messages, events and so on. However, the latest iOS truly embraces the concept of notifications, and the system introduced in iOS 5 features an enhanced suite to allow you to tailor all aspects of how your device gets messages to you.

Now, you are able to get messages, notifications, news and the latest scores delivered to the top of your screen without disturbing what you are currently doing. All you have to do in order to set up your own personalised Notification Center is go to Settings, choose the apps, and then select the order that they will appear in your Notification Center, and the manner in which they alert you. To stay in the loop, simply swipe down from the top of the screen, and you will be presented with a list of notifications for all of the apps that you have featured. In this guide, we will show you just how to get the most out of this fantastic feature.

Notification Center Set up Notification Center

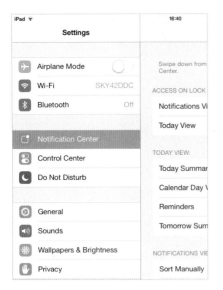

01 From your iPad's home screen, tap 'Settings', which is housed in your dock by default, the silver cog icon. Then tap on 'Notification Center', which should be the fourth option down on the list.

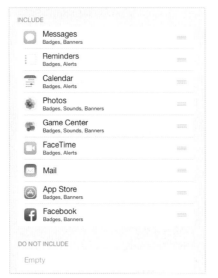

02 In Settings, you can choose which apps are featured in Notification Center. Tap 'Edit', then hold the right-hand edge of each app strip and drag it into position. The menu will automatically move other apps up or down the list.

03 Tap the arrow next to an app, and you will see options that are specific to that app. Choose how many items related to that app are displayed when a notification relating to it arrives. You can show up to ten items.

Badge icons
This slider will determine whether the icon for the app that is notifying you is displayed in the alert. It looks better if they are on

Different styles
There are three different types of alert styles for you to choose from. If you find 'Alerts' too intrusive, try using the banners option

View in lock screen
This option determines if alerts appear on your device's lock screen. It is good to have this activated so that you never miss a thing

Alert Style
You can decide how alerts are conveyed to you; either by the standard-style Alert, via a non-intrusive Banner, or no notifications at all

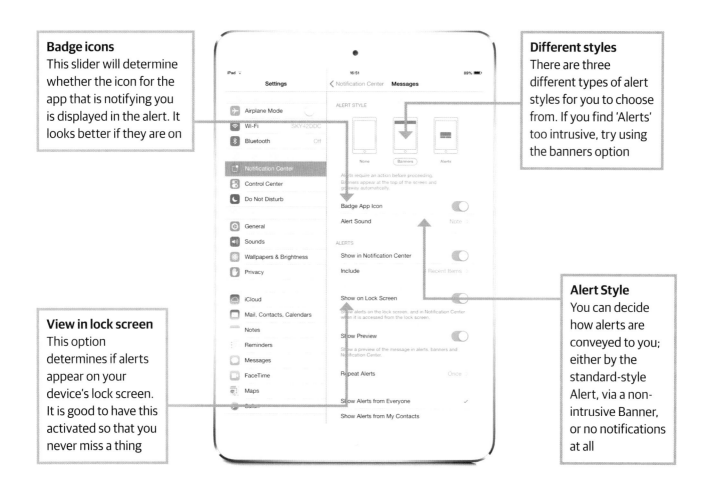

04 All you need to do is swipe down from the top of your iPad's screen to call up a window of notifications based on the options that you have selected. If you liked the old boxes, you can also select this option.

05 Notifications arrive in the form of a message at the top of the screen, and don't intrude with the app you are currently using, giving you the option to ignore it if you so wish. Swipe it up to dismiss it. You will find it in Notification Center.

06 If you need to respond to a notification immediately, tap it in your Notification Center or the banner at the top of the screen, and you will then be taken to the specific app in order for you to carry out your actions.

Manage contacts in FaceTime

Being able to make calls in FaceTime is easy, but you'll need to manage which contacts have it and how to get a hold of them

The first time you use FaceTime it might be surprising to see that the Contacts section is fully populated. It's because FaceTime uses the details in the Contacts app and this in turn can import all the contacts that you have in Outlook or your Mac's Contacts. Each time there's a sync with iTunes, the contacts are synchronised across all the apps. If you don't use Outlook or Contacts then – of course – the people in the Contacts folder will just be the ones you've added.

It isn't necessary to add or delete anything using FaceTime; you can do it in the Contacts app. As soon as anything is changed here it is reflected in the FaceTime app. Any changes will then be propagated back to the desktop program you are syncing contacts with to ensure conformity across all the software. Equally, any change to a contact in FaceTime is reflected in Contacts and then transferred back when syncing. In this tutorial though, we're going to import contacts from Outlook and manage them from within FaceTime.

"FaceTime can import all the contacts that you have in Outlook or Contacts"

FaceTime Managing your contacts

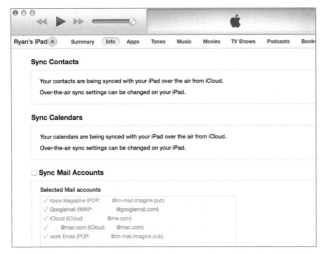

01 Head into your iTunes Library view and click on your device on the right-hand side of the top menu bar, then click onto the 'Info' tab. Now put a tick in the box that says 'Sync Contacts' at the top of the screen, and then choose to which contacts to add.

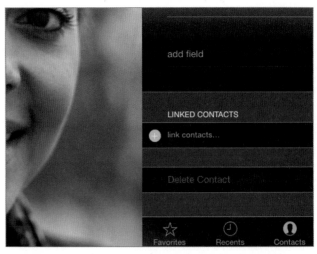

02 Perform a sync to add your desktop contacts to both the Contacts app and FaceTime. Tap on FaceTime and then Contacts. To delete a contact that you won't be needing any more, tap on the name of it, then 'Edit'. Scroll to the bottom and tap 'Delete Contact'.

Add an image
To give your contacts a more visual look, tap the 'Add Photo' button and either use the camera to take a picture or browse the Photo Library for one. You can then scale the image to fit inside the square

Change the tune
By default, all contacts will ring you with the same built-in ringtone which is the Strum noise. However, you can change this to any of the alarm noises by tapping on 'Ringtone'

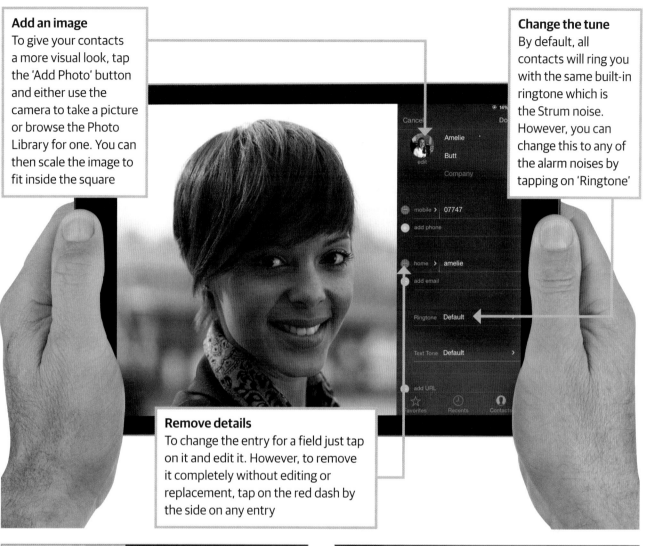

Remove details
To change the entry for a field just tap on it and edit it. However, to remove it completely without editing or replacement, tap on the red dash by the side on any entry

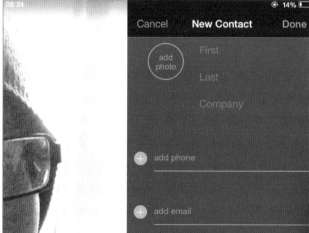

03 To add a new contact tap on the '+' symbol, located in the top right of the FaceTime interface. Enter all the details you have to hand then click on 'Add Photo'. Select to either take a photo or choose one from the Library. Once finished, click on 'Done'.

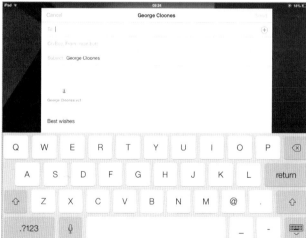

04 To share a contact with someone else, select the contact in question and then tap on 'Share Contact'. Type in the email address of the person to share the contact with, write your message and click on 'Send'. All the contact details will now be emailed to that person.

Make calls using FaceTime

It's one of the most exciting features of the iPad; the ability to make video calls. Here we should you how to do exactly that

The addition of dual cameras to the iPad 2 was one of the worst kept secrets and yet it was also one of the most anticipated features of the device's launch. Not so much for the ability to go out and take pictures with your iPad, as the large device is not exactly built for this purpose, but instead for apps that handle video calling, capture and transmission.

Yes, FaceTime arrived on the iPad. If you're used to an iPhone then this is slightly different. The cameras are the same resolution, so if you think your main screen image looks soft, it's because it's being displayed at the huge iPad size, not a tiny iPhone size.

The first thing you need to have in place before any calls are made is to register FaceTime using your Apple ID. This is the ID that is used by Apple and the App Store for purchases. Once the Apple ID is set up for the FaceTime account then an email address needs to be assigned to it. This is the one that you will use to call other people and that they will use to call you. Let's take a look.

"Before any calls are made, you must register FaceTime using your Apple ID"

FaceTime Register FaceTime and make calls

01 To register your details, tap on the Settings app and scroll down the list of built-in apps until you get to FaceTime. Tap on this and toggle FaceTime On. You will be required to enter your Apple ID. Enter the email address and the password and then tap 'Sign In'.

02 FaceTime can use different email addresses. Enter the one that you would like to use for your calls. If it's the same as your Apple ID account, it will be verified immediately. However, if it is a different email address, a verification link will be sent to that address.

Cameras in use
When activating FaceTime for a call, the first thing you see is yourself. When FaceTime connects the call, this window shrinks to a postage size so you can still see yourself and this main window fills with the video from the contact

Mute calls
The mic icon will mute the sound from your end of the call. This is useful if you need to talk to people off camera. Simply click on the same icon again to restore the sound as normal

Switch camera
By tapping this icon you will switch cameras so that instead of seeing your face, the person you are calling will see what you are pointing your iPad at. Good for showing off items

End call
Once your call is finished with, tap on the middle red button to hang up. During your call the buttons will fade so tap the screen to wake them up..

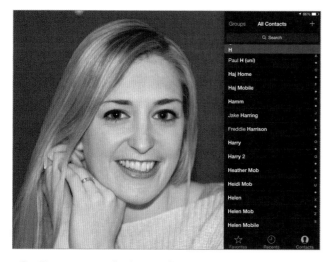

03 Once verified, your details will be displayed and FaceTime will be on. Exit Settings and tap on the FaceTime app. This will show the display from the front-facing camera. Then simply tap on the Contacts box found at the bottom in order to list them.

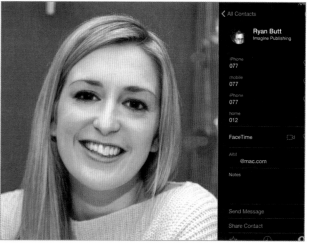

04 Tap on the person whom you would like to call. If they have a FaceTime account then they will have a FaceTime option beneath their phone number. Tap on either the video camera to make a FaceTime call, or the phone to make a FaceTime Audio call.

Use Messages to keep in contact

Get to grips with Apple's built-in messaging service and send unlimited text messages to your friends

With iOS 8, it has never been easier to stay in touch with your friends and family using your Apple device. Thanks to the Messages app and the iMessage service (that you need to activate in Settings> Messages), you can send unlimited text messages to everyone you know over Wi-Fi, 3G or 4G.

Through the app you can share photos, videos, locations and contacts around your social circles, and keep everyone in the loop via group messaging. To start, tap the 'New Message' button, and enter the Apple ID of the people you wish to contact. Then simply enter words into a text field, hitting the camera button to attach media,

and tapping 'Send'. It's free, so as long as your friends have iOS 5, 6, 7 or 8 installed, you can text without worrying about incurring a hefty bill. All messages can be tracked with delivery receipts, and thanks to the iCloud, you can start a conversation on one device, and finish it later on another. Here's an introduction to the service.

Messages How to text for free

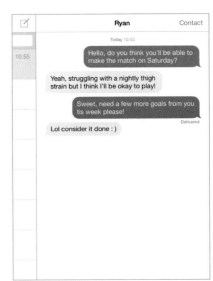

01 To kick things off you will need to tap the New Message icon (a piece of paper and a pen), and you will then be prompted to enter the Apple ID of the person you wish to send a message to.

02 Tap on the text field and type your message into the window. There are no text restraints. When you have finished writing what you wish to say in your email, select the 'Send' option and your message will be delivered.

03 The conversations will be neatly displayed in the main window. The text will be colour-coded – blue will be your message and grey the recipient. To swap conversations tap on the contact's name on the left.

Your recipients
All of your friends will be listed in the column to the left of the window. You can bring in more people for group conversations

Delete messages
Delete messages by holding on the message and choosing 'More'. Now select the message and tap on the trash icon

Adding photos
Images and videos can be added and attached to your messages. Just type your message, and then tap the camera icon to select and send media

Instant messaging
Sending messages is easy; just tap on the text field, type what you want and hit the 'Send' button. Each text bubble is colour-coded to make it easy to see who said what

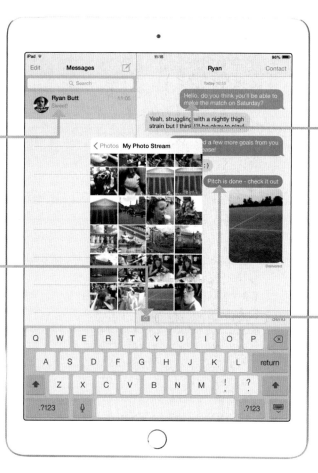

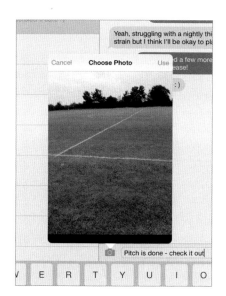

04 Once you have typed your message, tap the camera icon, pick a photograph you wish to send from your Camera Roll, and then tap 'Use' to include it in your next message. Your contact will then be able to open the image.

05 Messages works alongside your Notification Center, so if you receive any new messages you will be instantly notified and can then be taken straight to the app to reply. Messages is also located at the bottom of the home screen.

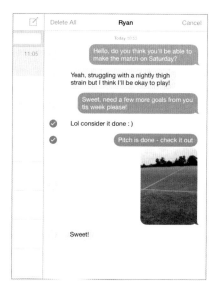

06 If there are parts of conversations you want to delete, press and hold on the message then tap 'More'. You can now select messages to delete. Once selected, tap the trash icon. The messages will then be deleted.

Instantly respond to notifications

If you receive a message or email, there is no need to leave the app you are in to deal with it; here's an alternative method

Your iPad can be used as a great communicative tool, but what happens if you receive important emails while you're in the middle of doing something else on your device? Not a problem, because by tailoring Notification Center, you can respond to notifications without ever leaving the app that you're in.

To get started, launch your Settings app from the Home screen and tap on the Notifications section in the left-hand column. You will see all of the apps in your Notification Center (which is normally accessible by swiping down from the top of the screen), so tap on one, such as Messages, and then ensure that the Allow Notifications slider is moved

to the On position and then select how you wish the notifications to appear on screen, such as Banners. Now, whenever you receive a new message, a banner alert will appear at the top of the screen to notify you. You can either launch the respective app to read and respond to the message, or swipe down on the message to read it and reply.

Notification Center Deal with notifications instantly

01 Launch the Settings app from your Home screen and go to the Notifications section. Ensure services such as Messages and Mail are included and set the alert style to Banners so that they appear at the top of the screen.

02 Now, when you receive messages, non-intrusive banner notifications will flash up at the top of the screen. If you ignore them they will vanish, but if you see that it needs an urgent response you can tap on it and pull down.

03 Pulling down on the notification provides a means of responding to the message no matter which app you are currently in. As you will see, a text field will appear into which you can write your response, so tap on this.

Instantly respond to notifications

Message notification
With your Notification Center settings configured correctly, banner alerts will appear at the top of the screen when you receive new messages

Speak your response
To make replying to messages easier you can do it hands-free. Tap on the microphone icon and speak your response to have it converted into text

Reply instantly
Pull down on the message notification to bring up the option to reply. Here you can add a subject and body text without leaving the app you are in

Predictive responses
The system is clever enough to provide quick responses based on the content on the message. Tap one of these to make responding quicker

04 Use the keyboard to enter a response and tap on the Send button to fire back the response. You can continue what you were previously doing with very little distraction, safe in the knowledge that your response has been sent.

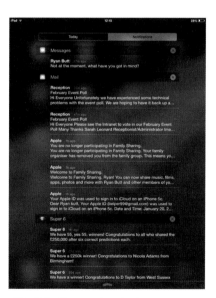

05 If you miss the banner notifications, you can still respond to messages and emails from your Notification Center. To access this, simply swipe down from the top of the screen, no matter which app you are currently in.

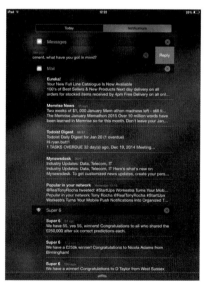

06 Tap on Notifications to see messages and emails and then swipe to the left on any entry to see options to Reply (for messages), Mark as Read or Archive (for emails). Close up the Notification Center by swiping up.

85

Send audio messages

Spice up the messages you send by sending your contacts audio clips rather than static text messages

When iOS 8 was introduced, Apple did a brilliant job with adding some new features to its oldest apps. For example, gone are the days where messages are simply visual. You can wave goodbye to boring texts and static images; the age of the quick and easy audio message is here. You never have to worry about leaving awkward voice mails or relying on your contacts to pick up when you're calling them from

a concert. They can simply pick the message up at any time that suits them and not miss out.

It's a really simple process that we take you through here. You start off by recording your message from within Messages, so there's no need to leave the app to record your message and awkwardly attach it. All

you have to do is hit the button and away you go.

What's more, your recipient can save the audio file once they have it so they can keep it on their device. If you're receiving the clips, you don't need to worry about them taking up space as you can choose whether or not you save the message.

"There's no need to leave the app to record your message and attach it"

Messages Send your friends audio clips

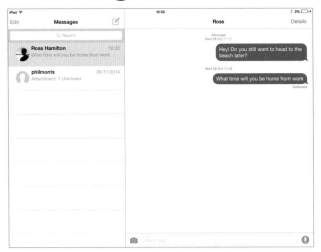

01 Head into the iMessage app and then open up a text stream with a contact or create a new message by tapping the New icon found in the top right-hand corner. This is where you will create your audio message.

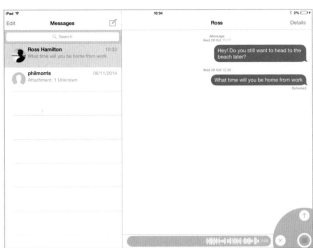

02 In order to record your message, look down at the bottom-right of the screen. To the right of the text input box you will see a circular icon with a microphone icon inside it. To record, hold down on the icon and speak your message.

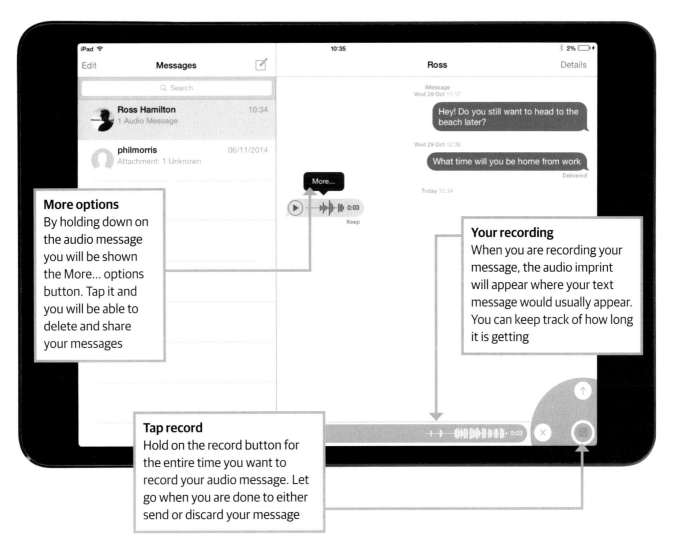

More options
By holding down on the audio message you will be shown the More... options button. Tap it and you will be able to delete and share your messages

Your recording
When you are recording your message, the audio imprint will appear where your text message would usually appear. You can keep track of how long it is getting

Tap record
Hold on the record button for the entire time you want to record your audio message. Let go when you are done to either send or discard your message

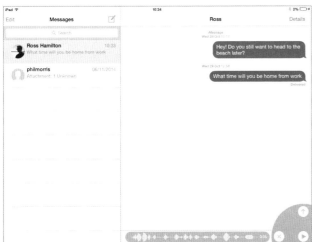

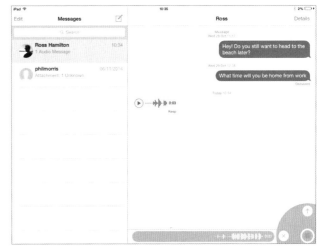

03 Hold the icon until you are finished with your message. When you are done, tap on the up arrow in order to send your message to your contact. When they have listened to it, you will be notified. If they save the message, it will tell you that as well.

04 If somebody sends you a message that you would like to save, when the audio message appears, simply tap on the message and the options shall appear. Tap on Save Message and it will now be saved to your iPad.

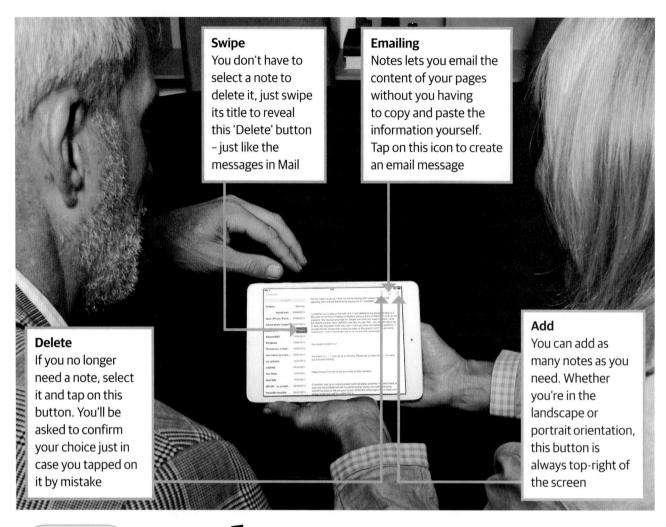

Swipe
You don't have to select a note to delete it, just swipe its title to reveal this 'Delete' button – just like the messages in Mail

Emailing
Notes lets you email the content of your pages without you having to copy and paste the information yourself. Tap on this icon to create an email message

Delete
If you no longer need a note, select it and tap on this button. You'll be asked to confirm your choice just in case you tapped on it by mistake

Add
You can add as many notes as you need. Whether you're in the landscape or portrait orientation, this button is always top-right of the screen

Make notes on your iPad

Don't feel you need to use a full word-processing suite in order to jot down ideas – you can do this just as easily with the built-in Notes app

Despite the fact that some people view the iPad as a device designed merely to consume media, just spending a few minutes with it will make you realise that this isn't true. With the help of a few choice programs, the iPad is capable of being used to create drawings, edit photos or

write essays. But you don't need to purchase anything for the latter, as the Notes app comes bundled with the iPad and is a really great place to start exploring how you can handle typing on glass.

Notes is remarkably similar to the program bearing the same name on the iPhone and iPod touch, it

has simply been expanded a little to take advantage of the additional space the iPad screen provides, and ultimately easier to use because of the bigger keys. This step-by-step tutorial will show you how it works, what you can do with it, and how it could help you in your regular day-to-day activities.

Notes Use Notes to write down ideas

01 Hold your iPad in the landscape orientation and open up the Notes app. Tap on the screen to reveal the keyboard. Now you can begin typing in your very first iPad note.

02 When you have finished, tap on the keyboard symbol with the down arrow (bottom-right of the keyboard) to dismiss it, then tap on the '+' button in the top-right of the interface.

03 That last action created a brand new note. You can swap between the first one and the one you're currently working on by selecting them from the column on the left.

04 All of your created notes will be displayed in the list to the left of the screen and they are all presented in the chronological order in which you created them, showing their creation date.

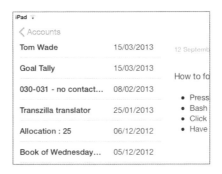

05 Whichever note is currently selected is highlighted in yellow in the list. You can swipe down to reveal more notes, if you have them stored on your device.

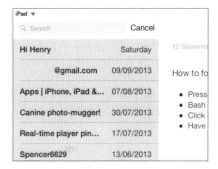

06 There's also a search field at the very top of the notes list, which can help you narrow down your search when you happen to be looking for any specific information. Just type in your terms.

07 Turn the iPad to the portrait orientation. You'll lose the permanent list (you can bring it back by swiping from the left), and you will now have a full view of your note.

08 If you type in a web link, it'll become active as soon as you hide the keyboard. Tap on it and you'll be sent to Safari. Tapping an email address sends you to Mail.

09 Notes recognises phone numbers. You're offered the options to 'Create New Contact' or 'Add To Existing Contact' instead. For places, you can 'Open in Maps'.

Get to know the Maps app

Learn to navigate your way around the iPad's Maps app, and let it lead the way wherever you go,

Ever since the iPhone and the iPad first launched, Google has provided the mapping experience on iOS. Now, since the release of iOS 6, Apple has struck out on its own and created an app from the ground up. They started completely from scratch when they began designing the app, and along with data from Yelp and TomTom,

they've created a beautiful application with some amazinglly useful features.

Maps now includes turn-by-turn navigation, effectively transforming your device into a satellite navigation system. With a 3D view and Siri integration on the new iPad, you can simply tell it where you want to go and hear

the instructions read back to you. The new app also includes a 3D view for major cities around the world; when you're viewing a city in the top-down view, dragging two fingers upwards will allow you to fly through the city and pan around in 3D. We've taken a look at all the brilliant new features below, so read on to find out more.

Maps The Maps app

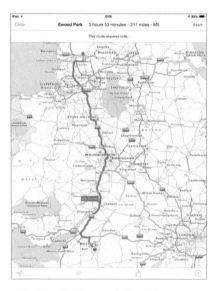

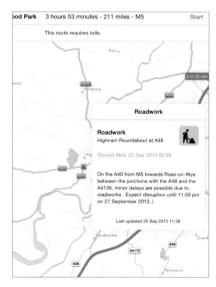

01 With the help of Yelp, there are now over 100 million added points of interest around the world – tap one and this informative window will appear showing a range of information and extra options.

02 In the top-left of the screen is the 'Directions' button. Tap it and enter your locations and you can then get directions instantly – if you're using one of the most recent iPad models then you will get a satnav-style 3D view.

03 The TomTom data also includes updates on any traffic problems. Tap an icon and you can view the time and details for each hold-up, enabling you to plan your journey around it. A very useful feature for every journey.

3D mode
To move into 3D mode you can either drag two fingers upwards to change the angle, or tap the 3D button in the bottom-left to change it automatically

Re-aligned
If you rotate the map with two fingers, you can realign the map to face north by tapping the compass icon in the top-right of the map

Location data
The app still allows you to find your current location using the button in the bottom-left, with your location shown as a blue dot

View options
Tap the fold in the bottom-right and you will see more options. You can view the map in different ways or show or hide traffic

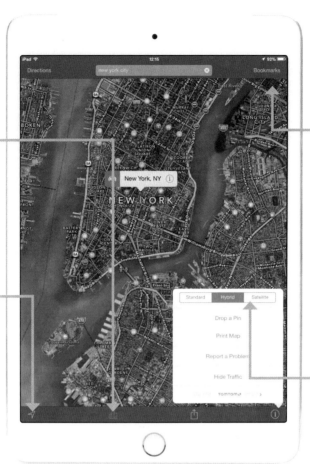

04 Since iOS 7, in the Maps app you can no longer zoom out to the extend of seeing the entire globe, but you can zoom out to see most of the world on one screen, then you can simply swipe to scroll around it.

05 Just like in Google Maps, your recent searches will be saved to the app's Bookmarks menu. You can also find your contacts and bookmarked locations included here, making regular searches easy to find.

06 Unlike Google Maps, the Maps app lets you use two fingers to twist the map around. This is perfect if you're following directions or need to get your bearings. This also saves on auto-rotation throwing you off.

91

Navigate using turn-by-turn

Apple's Maps is a great way to get from A to B, without having to take your eyes off the road

Maps are vital when it comes to finding your way around a strange town. But it's harder when you're finding your way around in a car. Unless you have a navigator next to you, reading a map can be a very dangerous activity.

This fact makes Apple's Maps app, which offers spoken turn-by-turn navigation, a huge boon. Set a departure point before you travel – Maps can even work out your current location – and a destination, and Maps will work out the most efficient way of getting you there. The app plots your progress to provide spoken and visual instructions as you go along the route. Your route will continue to be tracked even if you open another app, and it still works on the iPad's lock screen.

While turn-by-turn directions only come on iPad 2 or later, equipped with 3G services, Maps is still useful in these circumstances. It will still track your location and provide on-screen directions without the audio announcements.

Maps Planning the best route

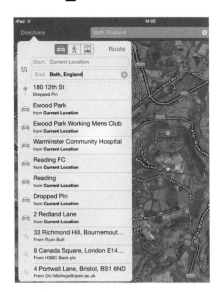

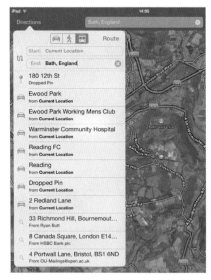

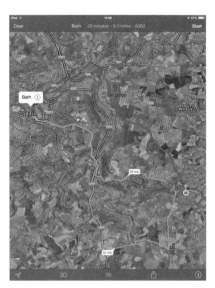

01 Open up the Maps app on your iPad and tap the 'Directions' button at the top-left of the screen. Then In the pop-up window, choose your mode of transport – take your pick of car, walking or bus.

02 Choose your journey's start and end points. You will have the option to select recent locations that you have entered into Maps, and choose your current location, or the location from which you will be travelling.

03 Tap the 'Route' button and Maps calculates the quickest journey route for you. Often the app will give you a choice between two or more routes and you can select which one you want to take.

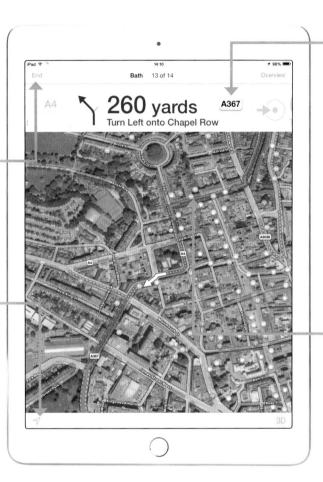

No mapping needed
Had enough of the route? Just tap here to end turn-by-turn navigation and return to the standard Maps view

Get your location
To use Maps to track your journey, you'll need to turn on Location Services for the Maps app. This can be easily found in Settings>Privacy

Instructions
Directions to your destination appear in the same design as road signs: clear and obvious, it's very easy to follow these instructions

Standard view only
Maps normally gives you the option of a satellite or hybrid views. But not in turn-by-turn mode, which offers a simpler standard view

04 Tap the 'Start' button at the top-right of the interface and Maps will display navigation instructions on screen. The app will also speak them to you as you travel on your route, much like a normal satnav.

05 Sometimes when you're navigating, it helps to get the bigger picture: tap the 'Overview' button to see the entire route on the screen, it'll give you context of where you're heading. Tap 'Resume' to return to the journey.

06 At any point you can tap the 'List' button at the bottom of the screen while in Overview. This will then display a text description of your route which lists each stage of your journey and the distance.

Use Voice Control on your iPad

Your iPad comes with all the benefits that Siri has to offer, and it's time to discover just how useful it can be

Apple's decision to bring Siri to the iPad was initially greeted with scepticism by those who could not see a use for such a feature on a tablet. However, the advantages do become clear the moment you start to use it. Over time, though, Siri has been improved beyond recognition and you can now ask Siri for help with a multitude of tasks, from the everyday to the more obscure.

From checking local film times to finding a local establishment, it is all there, and the process to use these features is simple. Siri even has a sense of humour, as you will find out if you ask Siri what it looks like, or ask for the meaning of life.

It seems as though Apple listened to the main criticisms of the earlier iOS versions too because Siri now has a dedicated page with much more space to display your various results, all of which you can tap on to display more.

So although a wave of cynicism may have greeted the idea of Siri when it was launched, it is definitely here to stay on the iPad.

"Siri now has a dedicated page with more space to display your various results"

Siri Get to grips with Siri

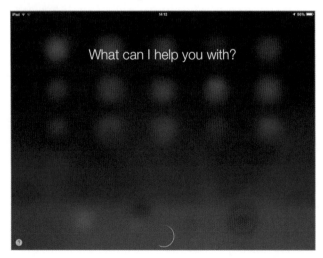

01 To launch Siri all you need to do is hold down the home button and it will pop up. You will hear a beep and the microphone will appear, this is your indicator to start speaking. If you have ticked the option in Settings, you can also access it from the lock screen.

02 You can now ask Siri any question you like. If you have waited a while, tap the microphone and ask your question. The answer can come back in different forms depending on what you asked, eg reference questions they usually come back visually.

Your details
Siri works best if it knows your personal details and these will come in handy time and time again. You could say 'Take me home' and the Maps app will know where that is. You can also call relatives simply by stating their relationship to you

Be completely natural
You can ask Siri questions in just the same way you would with another person. The software has been designed to understand the vagaries of language and feels much less computerised than many other voice recognition solutions

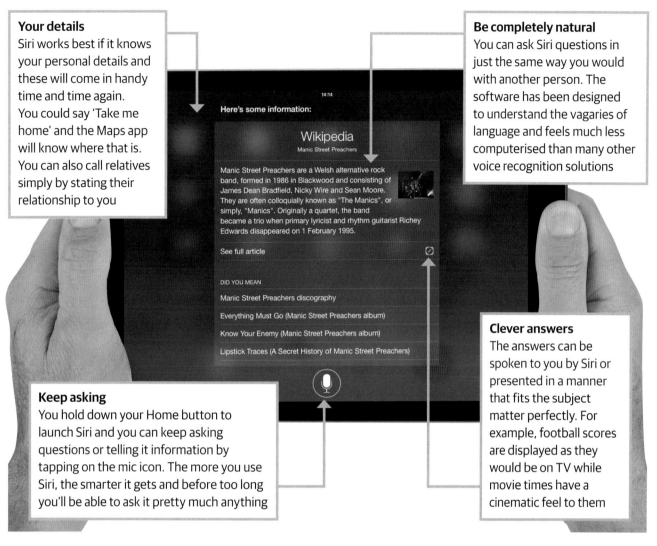

Here's some information:

Wikipedia
Manic Street Preachers

Manic Street Preachers are a Welsh alternative rock band, formed in 1986 in Blackwood and consisting of James Dean Bradfield, Nicky Wire and Sean Moore. They are often colloquially known as "The Manics", or simply, "Manics". Originally a quartet, the band became a trio when primary lyricist and rhythm guitarist Richey Edwards disappeared on 1 February 1995.

See full article

DID YOU MEAN

Manic Street Preachers discography

Everything Must Go (Manic Street Preachers album)

Know Your Enemy (Manic Street Preachers album)

Lipstick Traces (A Secret History of Manic Street Preachers)

Keep asking
You hold down your Home button to launch Siri and you can keep asking questions or telling it information by tapping on the mic icon. The more you use Siri, the smarter it gets and before too long you'll be able to ask it pretty much anything

Clever answers
The answers can be spoken to you by Siri or presented in a manner that fits the subject matter perfectly. For example, football scores are displayed as they would be on TV while movie times have a cinematic feel to them

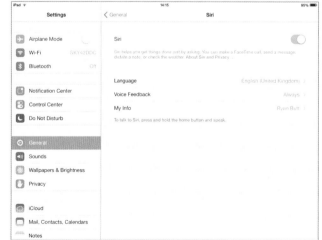

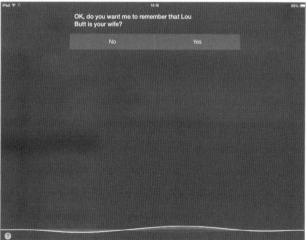

03 In Settings>General>Siri you can choose whether to activate the service or not and to specify your language as well. The 'My Info' section is important and you should make sure that you have a contact set up for yourself with all of your relevant information detailed.

04 If you have contacts for your partner, children, and so on, it is worth telling Siri how these relate to you. Once you have, you can say things like 'Message my wife' in the future and Siri will know exactly who to contact. It makes communicating from your iPad quicker.

Master voice control

Siri is now more capable, natural and flexible than ever before and works on any iPad

Siri has always been very flexible and natural to use, but it received some improvements in the previous iOS 7 to make it even smoother. A host of new features became available such as the ability to play back your last voicemail and to increase or decrease the screen brightness. Siri also deals with pronunciations much more effectively and really does sound more human than ever. No matter what aspects of Siri you like to use a simple hold of the home button will enable it ready for your questions or commands. It interacts with Twitter and almost all of the built in apps so that you can effectively use your iPad with only the occasional touch needed. The best advice we can give is to not think about what Siri can do, but to presume it can do everything. Ask it any question and you may be surprised at what it is capable of. From movie times to driving directions to general web queries, Siri will help you every minute of every day, and the more you use it the better it gets.

Siri Understanding Siri

01 If you hold down the home button on your iPad, then the screen will fill up with the Siri interface and a nice greeting to get you started and underway. Ready to answer any questions or queries you may have.

02 Ask Siri a simple question such as when your next appointment is. Siri will present a calendar entry which you can tap to adjust, showing you what you have entered into the calendar on your tablet.

03 Since iOS 7 Siri can interact more deeply with settings. You can ask to increase the brightness, lock the rotation, turn on Wi-Fi or Bluetooth as well as the original features, answering your questions and finding places.

Multiple app interaction
Siri can create reminders, set alarms and send messages with ease. It can interact with many of the built in iPad apps

Use the button
Hold down the home button wherever you are on your iPad. Siri will pop up even when you are in another app or game

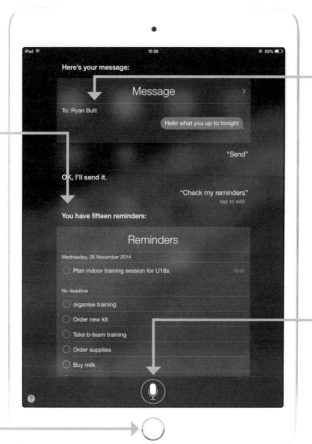

Deal with relationships
All Siri needs is one contact card to know who the closest people to you are. It will then understand your descriptions for each person

Find anything
If Siri does not support a query directly it will do a web search to provide results from a potential list of millions of answers

04 It is surprising what Siri knows. Ask what films are playing locally to receive trailers, reviews and exact film times for nearby cinemas. Siri will even get you directions and show you the map.

05 You can now ask for currency exchange rates. Siri will be able to recognise common currencies such and pounds and dollars, then provide with all the information you could possibly need!

06 We have been able to tweet from Siri for a while, but now it's possible to see what's trending on the popular social network service. Just remember, you only need to ask and Siri will answer.

Post to Twitter with Siri

Don't type social networking messages when you can just speak your posts with Siri

Siri is an amazing assistant built into the iPad and it is capable of carrying out an incredibly wide range of commands. All you have to do is to press the Home button for a couple of seconds and then say what you want it to do. If you have installed and set up the Twitter and Facebook apps on the iPad, you can easily post Twitter messages and add

Facebook updates simply by saying what you want. Saying 'tweet' is sufficient to display an empty Twitter message with Siri listening intently for you to speak whatever you want to post. Similarly, 'post to facebook' will display a Facebook box ready to convert your speech into a status update, which will go live as soon as you request.

In this tutorial we have broken down the procedure into short steps, but once you get the hang of it, you can experiment with more complex commands and take shortcuts. For example, you can string together two or more commands, like 'Post to Facebook…'. Everything after 'Facebook' becomes the post. Try it and see.

Siri Speak your Facebook updates

01 To kick things off, hold down the home button at the bottom of your iPad until the Siri microphone icon appears on the screen. Siri will then start listening for commands after a couple of seconds.

02 Say 'tweet' and Siri displays an empty Twitter message box, but say 'post to Facebook' and an empty Facebook message appears. Siri will then listen for the message to add once you start narrating.

03 Say the message you want to post and after a few seconds Siri will turn it into text and insert it into the post body automatically for you. Say the word 'Send' or tap the 'Send' option and Siri uploads it.

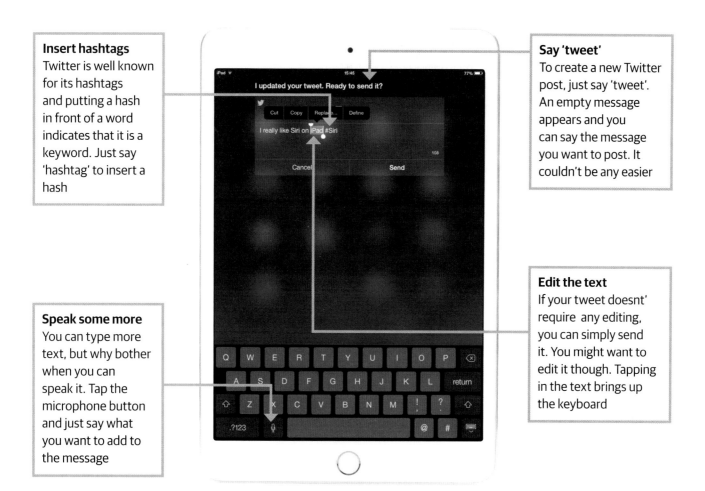

Insert hashtags
Twitter is well known for its hashtags and putting a hash in front of a word indicates that it is a keyword. Just say 'hashtag' to insert a hash

Say 'tweet'
To create a new Twitter post, just say 'tweet'. An empty message appears and you can say the message you want to post. It couldn't be any easier

Edit the text
If your tweet doesnt' require any editing, you can simply send it. You might want to edit it though. Tapping in the text brings up the keyboard

Speak some more
You can type more text, but why bother when you can speak it. Tap the microphone button and just say what you want to add to the message

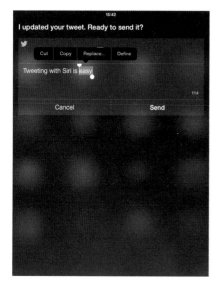  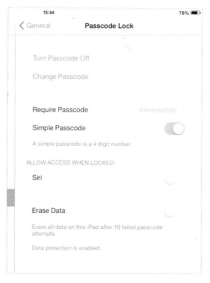

04 This step is entirely optional and is only required if you want to change the text of the message in some way. Tap anywhere inside the message body and a keyboard is displayed ready for your changes.

05 This is another optional step and if you want to, you can easily add more to the message. Press on the microphone button on the keyboard and narrate whatever you want to add to the text.

06 Mischievous friends can pick up your iPad and post to Facebook and Twitter! To block this, go to Settings>General>Passcode Lock and turn off Siri under 'Allow Access When Locked'.

Explore the App Store

The iPad's App Store underwent an exciting revamp with iOS 7. Learn how to navigate the App Store and open up a world of possibility

As part of the huge iOS 7 update, all Apple mobile stores received a substantial make-over. The new App Store was tweaked and enhanced in order to produce a more efficient user experience, and it has certainly succeeded. The App Store on your iPad is now easier than ever to navigate and purchase items from.

Of the new features, perhaps the most significant is being able to download new apps inside the App Store, rather than being taken to one of your home pages. There's also a new intuitive Genius bar to give you clever recommendations.

Other new features include being able to view each app's update history, as well as individual developer pages. Facebook integration is also present, while the ability to view app screenshots in full screen is a big positive.

This is definitely not an upgrade to worry about, but one to embrace. All your favourite options remain, but most have received a little bit of Apple's magic dust. Let's have a closer look at four of the most important changes.

"The App Store on your iPad is now easier than ever to navigate"

App Store So what's new?

01 The biggest change to the App Store is based on purchasing new apps. Instead of being whisked away to your home screen from the app when you hit the buy button, you can now watch the installation process inside the App Store itself. It's a welcome addition!

02 A new feature of the App Store is Near Me. Tap on this at the bottom of the interface and then you can opt to display apps that are popular near your current location. It's particularly useful for finding apps for local companies and shops.

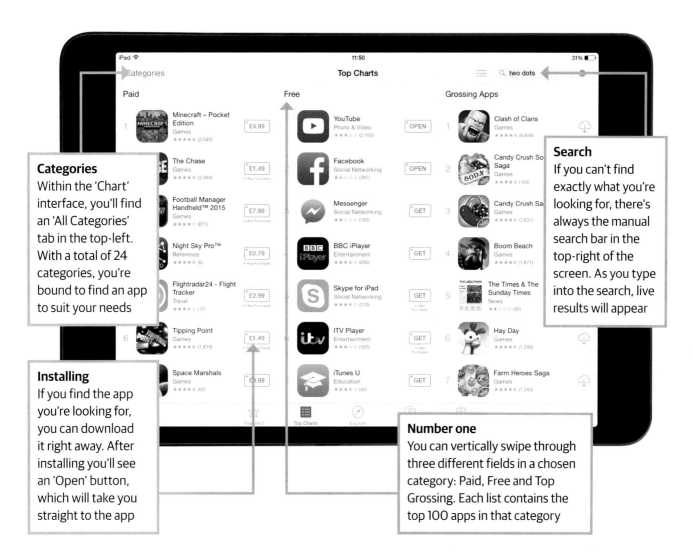

Categories
Within the 'Chart' interface, you'll find an 'All Categories' tab in the top-left. With a total of 24 categories, you're bound to find an app to suit your needs

Installing
If you find the app you're looking for, you can download it right away. After installing you'll see an 'Open' button, which will take you straight to the app

Search
If you can't find exactly what you're looking for, there's always the manual search bar in the top-right of the screen. As you type into the search, live results will appear

Number one
You can vertically swipe through three different fields in a chosen category: Paid, Free and Top Grossing. Each list contains the top 100 apps in that category

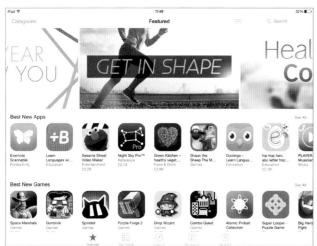

03 The new-style App Store has been built from the ground up. It's a comprehensive re-design that ultimately makes it easier than ever before to navigate. Menus can be intelligently swiped through, and it all looks perfect on the large real estate your iPad provides.

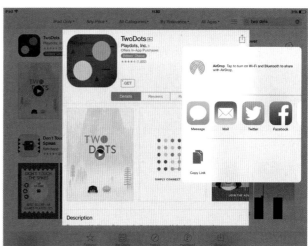

04 If you come across an app you're fond of, or one that you think everyone needs to know about, however well known, iOS 7 added a selection of sharing options for you to utilise. Simply hit the share icon to view your different options.

Check out the iTunes Store app

The iTunes Store is designed to make buying and downloading music that much easier

Much the same as the App Store, the iTunes Store has undergone a major design overhaul. Your iPad's screen size showcases the re-design perfectly. The added screen real estate is unbeatable. When you open up the new app, you will instantly be greeted by the latest and most popular options. New releases are showcased at the top and you now have the ability to browse with a swipe of your finger.

Of course, further iCloud integration ensures all your past purchases are up to date. You can start shopping on your iPhone and seamlessly check out over on your iPad. As part of the previous iOS 7 update, you can download songs, albums and films from iTunes without leaving the app. It's all part of making the buying process simpler than ever.

All the usual features remain untouched. This update is only a cosmetic one, but one that we're sure provides a much more intuitive user experience. Here's a quick overview of the features you need to know about.

> "You can now view a download's progress via a handy in-app status bar"

iTunes Shop till you drop

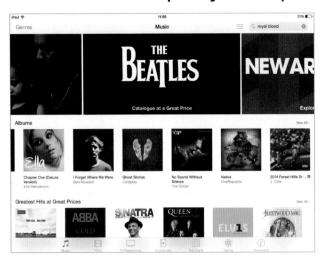

01 The first time you load the app, it will appear very different. Lots has changed, but it's all for the better. There are home pages for the different categories, and you can swipe through popular categories like top singles, albums and new releases.

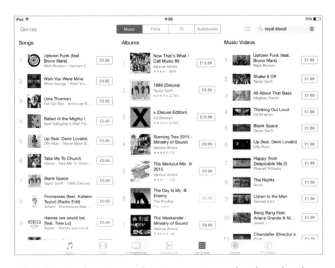

02 Each category has its most popular downloads listed under the Charts tab that you can find at the bottom of the app highlighted by a star symbol. The music section, for example, lets you vertically scroll through the top 100 songs, albums and music videos.

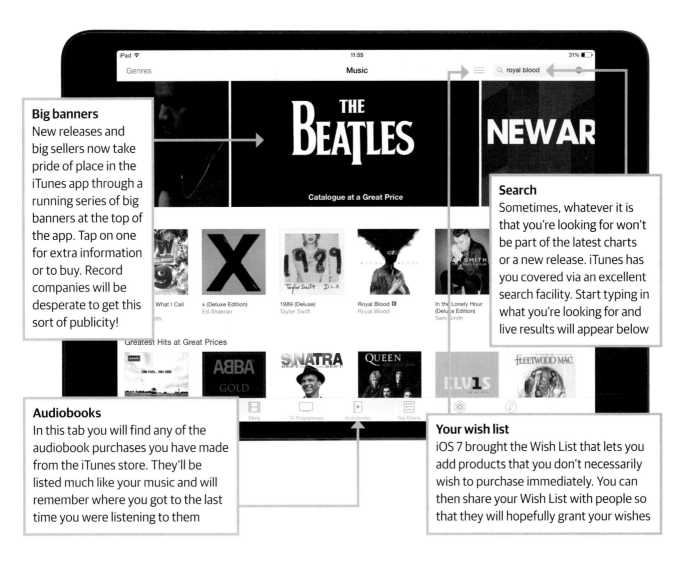

Big banners
New releases and big sellers now take pride of place in the iTunes app through a running series of big banners at the top of the app. Tap on one for extra information or to buy. Record companies will be desperate to get this sort of publicity!

Search
Sometimes, whatever it is that you're looking for won't be part of the latest charts or a new release. iTunes has you covered via an excellent search facility. Start typing in what you're looking for and live results will appear below

Audiobooks
In this tab you will find any of the audiobook purchases you have made from the iTunes store. They'll be listed much like your music and will remember where you got to the last time you were listening to them

Your wish list
iOS 7 brought the Wish List that lets you add products that you don't necessarily wish to purchase immediately. You can then share your Wish List with people so that they will hopefully grant your wishes

03 If you find something that you're interested in, a straightforward tap on its title will take you to a page packed with extra information. Do so with a film, and you'll find details such as trailers, ratings and reviews, and you'll have the ability to buy it by tapping its price.

04 Since the introduction of iCloud, all your pre-iCloud purchases can be viewed and downloaded on multiple devices. Hit the 'Purchased' tab and use the 'Not on this iPad' option to search for songs or an artist. To download a song, tap the cloud icon.

Featured content
All of the most recent, hottest releases will be displayed in the top area of the screen that appears when you first tap on each store section

Search for content
You can use the Genre tabs at the top of the screen to narrow down your search, or you can enter specific keywords into the Search engine to instantly find what you want

Store categories
All of the different store categories, such as Music, Films, TV Shows, etc, are displayed as icons along the bottom of the screen. Tap on one to access it

Previous
When you purchase a song, film or other media from iTunes, a Downloads tab will appear in the bottom-right. You can see their download progress by tapping on the icon here

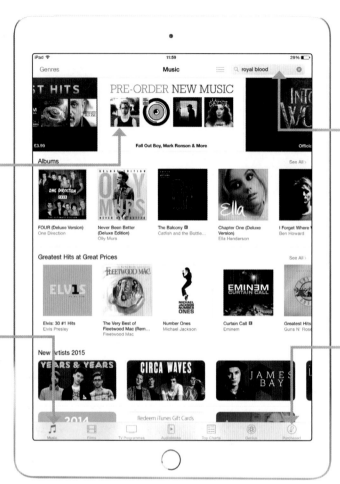

Use iTunes to download media

We show you how to use Apple's virtual superstore to purchase music, films and other assorted media

The birth of iTunes signalled a significant change in the way we shop for music and media. Everything can now be bought whenever and wherever we are and it's all thanks to iTunes.

The iTunes app for your iPad is a friendly and welcoming portal to a thriving online marketplace where you can shop at your leisure and

not be suckered into slinging cheap tat that is on display next to the tills into your basket. You go in, get what you want and, within minutes, be listening to it through your iPad's Music app or watching it through the Videos app. Using iTunes really couldn't be easier. Everything is well laid out and easily accessible and all of your past and present purchases

are with you at all times for when you need them. The hardest part, if there even is a hard part, is ensuring that all of your billing information is up-to-date and correct. Once it is, all of the songs and flicks you could ever want will be at your fingertips. Here we guide you through this essential app, so you can purchase music, movies and audiobooks with ease.

iTunes How to browse and buy media

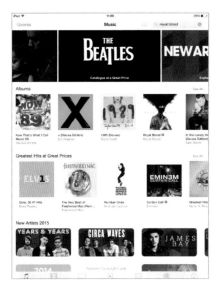

01 When you launch the iTunes app you will be taken straight to the main storefront, which is the Music Store by default. All of the categories in the store are laid out across the bottom of the screen for you to choose from.

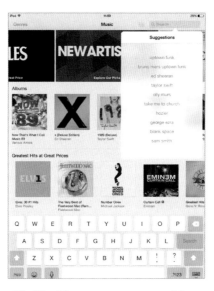

02 The newest, most exciting media will always be displayed on the main page. If you don't find what you want there then you can always search for specific artists and albums by using the 'Search' window.

03 When you find what you want, tap on it to bring up a window for that artist or album. Then tap the price at the top to buy the entire album, or tap on the price next to the separate tracks to download them individually.

04 After opting to download an item you will be required to sign in using your Apple ID to authorise the purchase. You may also be required to enter billing information, depending on your Apple ID settings.

05 You can also purchase films, TV shows and audiobooks through iTunes. The main difference between these types of media is that with movies you can choose to rent, as well as buy your favourite titles.

06 The iTunes app is compatible with your personal iCloud account, so anything you purchase from the store can be automatically pushed to all of your other iOS devices free of charge. So enjoy your media on all your devices!

The next step

Get to grips with the iPad's more in-depth features with our guides

"Your iPad
can become a
hub for media"

Using your iPad's camera

When you need to capture a moment and you have your iPad with you, it is capable of everything you'll need

The iPad camera is not an obvious feature, mainly because of the size of the tablet itself, but if you happen to have it with you and want to grab a quick snap you may as well know how it all works. Despite specifications that are meagre in comparison to standalone cameras and some smartphones, it is still capable of capturing decent quality photos and videos if you take time to make it work properly. There are options for stills and video as you would expect as well as a Square option for capturing perfectly proportioned photos. These could be used for scanned documents or anything else and this simple addition of a unusual shape adds some charm to the experience. HDR will help you deal with unusual lighting and like everything else in the interface it is just one tap away at all times. Indeed, it is surprising how functional and fully featured iPad cameras are and since iOS 7, everything has been upgraded just a little to make the final results even better than before.

Camera iPad photos and videos

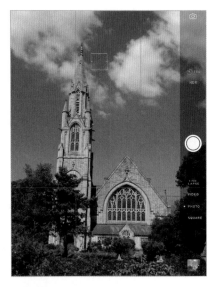

01 Tap the Camera icon and you will be presented with a different look in the main interface. Swipe along the right-hand bar to select the available options. Take your time to familiarise yourself with the different options.

02 Tap the screen where you would like it to focus and the lens will pinpoint on that particular spot. It is highlighted by a yellow square on the screen. This can be used to draw attention to a certain aspect of your photo.

03 Slide the right-hand bar down to go to video mode, and press the record button to start. When it's recording the capture button becomes a red square and a timer is displayed, so you can keep track of the length of your video.

The capture button
The capture button is logically placed for ease of use and will turn red when you are recording video. Hold it to take burst shots

See your snaps
Tap this small icon to quickly jump to your camera roll to see all of your photos. This is great for quickly checking your last shot

HDR
Turning the HDR option on is particularly helpful when you are taking landscape shots with varied light sources. It can greatly improve any photo

Square photos
Square photos are excellent for taking more serious photos such as scanning documents or trying to capture a passport photo. They also look quite retro

04 Tapping the top right-hand icon will swap to the front-facing camera, on the screen face of the iPad, which is useful if you want to take a picture of yourself. Alternatively, you could use this option as a mirror.

05 The HDR function works particularly well with landscape shots and scenery pictures and can help you capture shots in much better quality. Experiment with the different options to see which works best.

06 Go to Settings>Photos & Camera and you will be able to add a grid to the camera view and save a standard shot when snapping HDR photos. Adding a grid can help you angle your photos and frame them nicely.

Edit images in Photos

Make the most of your iPad's camera, and take advantage of the built-in photo-editing feature

Whereas taking photos on your iPad is quick and easy with the Camera app, organising and editing the photos that you take is equally as intuitive with the Photos app. All of the photos that you take are uploaded to your iCloud Drive and made available on all of your iOS devices and as you collection

grows, they will be neatly organised by date and location – and a built-in search facility makes it easy to find specific photos when you need them. What's more, you can make edits to photos within the Photos app to make them look as eye-catching as possible before sharing them with others. You can make smart adjustments

to all aspects of the photo with a single tap or really go to town fine tuning each individual aspect and even applying filters to turn seemingly standard images into fabulous works of art. Read on to discover how the Photos app can revolutionise your images to really make them stand out and be ready for sharing.

Photos Edit your photographs on your iPad

01 Launch the Photos app from the home screen, and you will automatically see all your pictures and videos sorted in order they were taken. Pick one you want to make amendments to, and then tap 'Edit'.

02 If you tap on the wand icon at the bottom of the screen the software will adjust the colours of the image. Tap the same option once again to cancel the changes or tap 'Done' to finish with your edit and save your changes.

03 Tapping the frame icon will allow you to crop the image by moving the corners of the frame or make adjustments to the orientation by rotating the dial at the bottom of the image so you can change the alignment.

Edit images in Photos

Enhance
On the surface this seems like a basic option compared to most dedicated editing packages, but in practice it's a great feature that can transform your photo within moments

Multi-touch controls
Before you choose how to edit a photo, you can use the multi-touch pinch controls to zoom in to the photo to focus on the areas you want to improve

Undo any changes
Thanks to the intuitiveness of the iPad, you can easily revert back to the original image by pressing cancel, and then quickly resave it

Crop photos
You can chop out parts of the photo (such as a blurred section or distraction) that you don't want anymore

04 If you wish to apply a filter effect to an image, tap on the filter icon and then swipe through the various options. Tap on one to preview what it looks like when applied to the image. There's plenty to choose from!

05 To make slight adjustments to the colour levels, tap on the dial icon, then choose the colour option, and move the slider across the long image at the bottom of make adjustments. You can see the results in real-time.

06 While making slight adjustments to the levels, tap the list icon to bring up more colour options, such as Exposure, Shadows and Contrast. Tap 'Done' to complete your edits. It will save to your photo stream.

Organise your photos

You can organise and keep all of your most important photos in order on an iPad with ease. It is logical and easy to do

Photos will always have a special place in our hearts, but it is very easy to take and collect so many that you often miss the truly special moments.

On an iPad and with the Photos app you have the ability to organise your collection logically and to ensure that the ones you view most often are always available. Some of the organisation can be done in iTunes on a Mac or PC connected to your iPad, but for quick tweaks and

for making changes on the move you have everything you need on the iPad to keep all of your photos in logical order. We will offer some tips on the most efficient and best ways to keep order and also demonstrate the steps you need to take, but there is nothing here that is difficult to understand or hard to remember.

The iPad is the perfect tool for viewing photos thanks to the superb screen and portable form. With its larger screen and capability to show more detail than other devices, you may well find that you prefer storing and viewing all your photos on your iPad rather than one your laptop or desktop computer.

> "The iPad is the perfect tool for viewing photos thanks to the superb screen"

Photos Manage your photo collection

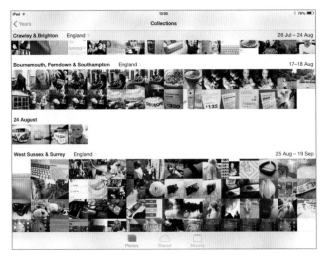

01 In iOS 8 all of your iPad photos are available to view by date using the 'Photos' icon at the bottom. They will be broken up by time and also by the location they were taken in and this is completely automatic. Tap the 'Albums' icon to continue.

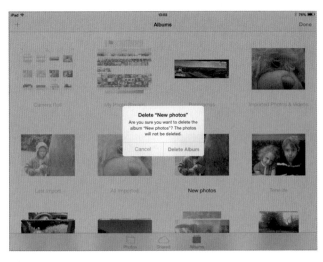

02 Most of your albums will be static and tapping the 'Edit' button will not enable changes, but some may show a small 'x' next to them. Tap this to delete an album. The photos within it will not be deleted and will remain available on the iPad.

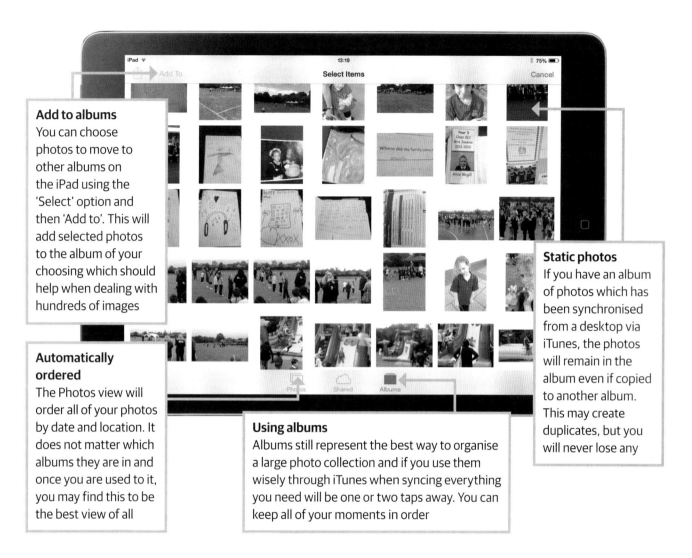

Add to albums

You can choose photos to move to other albums on the iPad using the 'Select' option and then 'Add to'. This will add selected photos to the album of your choosing which should help when dealing with hundreds of images

Automatically ordered

The Photos view will order all of your photos by date and location. It does not matter which albums they are in and once you are used to it, you may find this to be the best view of all

Using albums

Albums still represent the best way to organise a large photo collection and if you use them wisely through iTunes when syncing everything you need will be one or two taps away. You can keep all of your moments in order

Static photos

If you have an album of photos which has been synchronised from a desktop via iTunes, the photos will remain in the album even if copied to another album. This may create duplicates, but you will never lose any

03 When in the album view, tap the '+' icon top-left to create a new album. You will be asked to give it a name and you can then choose which photos you want to add to the album. The photos you add will still stay in their original albums as well.

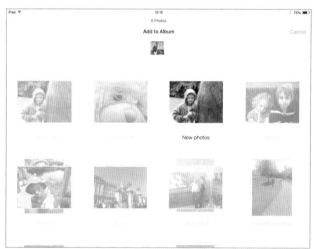

04 Tap the 'Select' option and then choose a few photos. Now tap the 'Add To' option top-left and you will be able to move the selected photos to a different album. As before, the original photos will remain in the album you have copied them from.

Get the most out of iPad videos

The iPad is perfectly designed for the mobile movie experience thanks to its large screen

The Videos feature alone has the potential to keep you occupied on long plane journeys, in hotels or waiting rooms, and adds a use to the iPad that could justify half of the cost straight away. It has been designed for ease of use, as most Apple software has, and takes care of many of the niggles found in competing devices. For example, it will automatically play a film from the point you left it, and expanding the screen requires just a simple double tap.

Everything is designed to help you get the most from the experience, but some tips are still useful to get you off to a flying start. In this step-by-step we will show you how to obtain new movies, how to transfer them to your iPad and how to make the most of the viewing experience. You could easily do all of this yourself, but in this instance a little knowledge certainly goes a long way and missing out on the movie capabilities of the iPad would be a real shame given the benefits it offers you.

> "It adds a use to the iPad that could justify half of the cost straight away"

Videos Make the most of movies

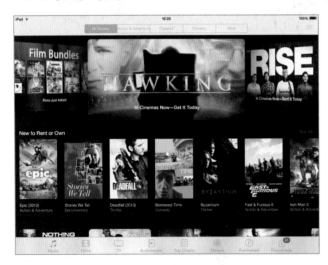

01 The easiest way to obtain the highest-quality content is via iTunes. Navigate to the 'Films' or 'TV Programmes' section of the store and choose the film you would like to rent or buy. The trailers are perfectly designed to give you an idea of content.

02 Your purchases will be downloaded and stored on your iPad. If you have iCloud activated then they will also automatically be pushed to your other devices wirelessly, such as your Mac or iPhone, allowing you to view them on those devices too.

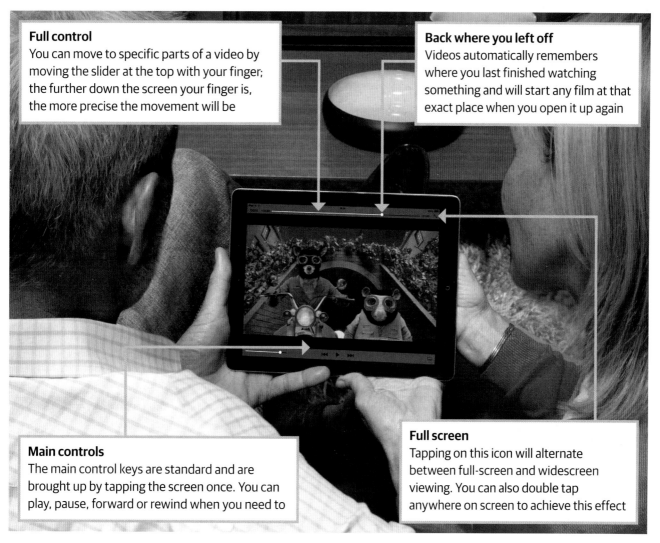

Full control
You can move to specific parts of a video by moving the slider at the top with your finger; the further down the screen your finger is, the more precise the movement will be

Back where you left off
Videos automatically remembers where you last finished watching something and will start any film at that exact place when you open it up again

Main controls
The main control keys are standard and are brought up by tapping the screen once. You can play, pause, forward or rewind when you need to

Full screen
Tapping on this icon will alternate between full-screen and widescreen viewing. You can also double tap anywhere on screen to achieve this effect

03 All you need to do now is simply tap the 'Videos' icon and choose the film you want to watch from the list of videos that you have installed on your iPad. The film (or TV programme, for that matter) will immediately start to play from the beginning.

04 Double-tapping the screen will make the movie fill the whole screen, and doing so again will take it back to standard format (which is useful for widescreen films). The rest of the on-screen tweaks are obvious in their implementation, such as play, pause, etc.

Get to know the Music app

We guide you around your iPad's Music app and show you how to make a playlist

Your iPad's Music app is your mobile music player and superstore all rolled into one. With a clean, simple, easy-to-manipulate interface that is great fun to play with, you can play any track stored in your library by tapping on it and using the playback controls; create your own Playlists on the fly; and even visit the iTunes Store from within the app to buy something new. It's the kind of thing makes you want to just sit there and spend an hour discovering new music.

What's more, if you have enabled your iCloud (the free cloud storage and syncing service that comes free with iOS 5 and above), any new music you purchase will be pushed to all of your iOS devices without you having to lift a finger. By the same process you can also access and download music that you have downloaded in the past at no cost.

In this tutorial we guide you through the intricacies of this versatile app and show you how to create Playlists, access your purchased music files and more.

Music Create a playlist

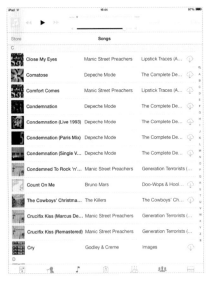

01 Your Music app can be found in your iPad's dock by default. To get started, tap on the icon to launch the app and then you will be able to discover the ease with which you can listen to music on your device.

02 Use the tiles at the bottom of the screen to browse your music by Playlist, Songs, Artists or Albums. Tap on a song of your choice to start playing it. The playback controls are at the top of the screen.

03 Tap on the Playlist tile and then tap 'New Playlist' in the top corner, as shown above. Then give your new Playlist a name, then add songs from your library, drag them into a preferred order and then tap 'Done'.

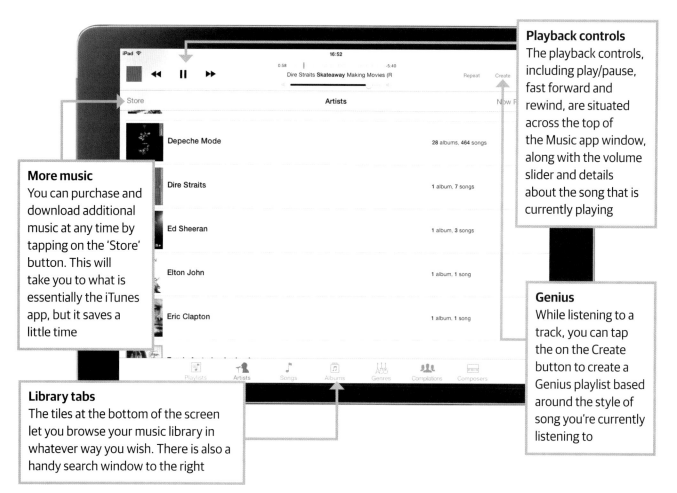

Playback controls
The playback controls, including play/pause, fast forward and rewind, are situated across the top of the Music app window, along with the volume slider and details about the song that is currently playing

More music
You can purchase and download additional music at any time by tapping on the 'Store' button. This will take you to what is essentially the iTunes app, but it saves a little time

Genius
While listening to a track, you can tap the on the Create button to create a Genius playlist based around the style of song you're currently listening to

Library tabs
The tiles at the bottom of the screen let you browse your music library in whatever way you wish. There is also a handy search window to the right

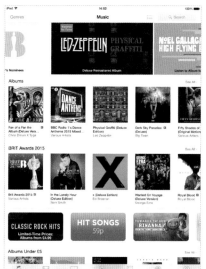

04 You can make new purchases from within the Music app by tapping the 'Store' button. You can then browse the full iTunes Store and download new music tracks, albums and podcasts, and search for what you want.

05 Through iCloud you can get all of your previous iTunes purchases beamed directly to your iPad, quickly and easily. Create an account and connect, then go to the 'Purchased' category in the iTunes Store.

06 Go to 'Settings' and then tap on 'Music' to access the app's preferences. Here you can set the EQ to the style of music you are playing, set a cap on how high the volume goes at any point, and much more.

Listen to podcasts on your iPad

Search for, subscribe to, and listen to fantastically immersive podcasts on your iPad

The iTunes store has recently become so big that it has had to migrate particular wings to their own standalone apps, such as iBooks, iTunesU and Podcasts. The Podcasts app will immediately have a very familiar look and feel to it.

Search the app by tapping the magnifying glass. When you find a suitable podcast, select it to view its info page and then tap on the 'Subscribe' button to ensure that your are notified as to when a new episode is ready for download. You can also tap on the cloud icons to download individual episodes.

To listen to your downloaded podcasts, tap on the My Podcasts icon and then select a podcast, followed by the episode. You will then be presented with a familiar set of playback controls to Play/ Pause and skip forward and back. You can also press, hold and drag the scrub bar at the bottom of the controls to fast track to a particular point in the episode. Even if you have never listed to a podcast before, this app makes it an enjoyable and intuitive experience.

Podcasts Download a podcast

01 Tap on the Featured icon and you will be taken to the Podcasts wing of the iTunes store where all of the latest podcasts will be displayed. Use the tabs to filter by Audio, Video or All to view both.

02 Tapping the Top Charts icon will list all of the podcasts that are currently popular. This is a good way to find content that is recent and that other users are listening to. You may even discover something new.

03 When you find a podcast that you would like to subscribe to, tap on the 'Subscribe' button and you will be notified whenever a new episode is ready to be downloaded and to be listened to.

Store tabs

Podcasts come in two flavours, Audio and Video, which are self-explanatory. Use the tabs at the top of the Featured store window to view the latest and greatest podcasts in each category. When you find one, hit 'Subscribe'

Your Podcasts

All of the podcasts that you have downloaded will be accessible through this section. Tap on a brand to view all of the podcasts inside and then tap an individual episode to start listening to it

Now playing

Like the Music app, if you currently have content playing then you will be able to access it via the 'Now Playing' link in the top-right corner and then access the playback controls to Play/Pause, skip and more

Search

If you have a good idea of the sort of content that you would like to download and listen to then tap on the Search icon and start entering keywords to find content that matches quickly and easily

04 You can also download individual episodes by tapping on the cloud icon next to a particular episode. All downloaded content will be accessible from the My Podcasts section of the app. See the next step!

05 When you are ready to start listening to a podcast, tap on the My Podcasts icon and select a podcast to listen to. Tap on an individual episode to start listening to it. It will be tagged with how many you have per series.

06 When you start listening to a podcast you will be presented with a familiar set of playback controls. You can also change the speed and use the scrub bar to jump to a particular point within the cast.

Listen to Genius playlists

Making your own special playlist is great but by letting the iPad do all the hard work you can get some really cool musical mixes

Keeping track of all the music on your iPad can be a bit of a pain. It's surprising how much music you can fit onto even just the 16GB version. With all that music it makes sense to keep track of it all and to create playlists.

Of course, listening to whole albums is fine, but then we all have our favourite tracks and like to hear them more often than others. Creating playlists manually is a great way of doing this, but it's time consuming and if you don't keep them updated they soon get rather tiresome.

You could just stick your whole music collection on random, but even this throws up issues like those hidden tracks or fillers that ruin a smooth transition, or the odd song you're getting bored of hearing. The best solution may well be Genius mixes.

Apple has created a tool that lets you select a track and automatically create a playlist of tracks that complement each other. It's a great way of keeping the music going around a certain theme and in the main it's incredibly reliable.

"We all have our favourite tracks and like to hear them more often than others"

Music Make Genius mixes on the iPad

01 Launch the Music application on your iPad. Your music can be displayed in a number of ways using the tabs along the bottom. Scroll until you find a song that would make a good foundation for your playlist; this will be the basis of your list.

02 When you have found a track that most suits your current mood, tap on it to start it playing. When you're ready, tap on the Create button in the top-right corner of the screen and then choose Genius Playlist from the pop-up menu that appears.

Controls
The iOS 7 update provided a complete new look for music on your iPad, and the basic controls can now be found up here in the top-left corner

Save your playlist
By clicking the 'Save' button you will store your new Genius playlist in the Music application on your iPad

Views
To view your music collection in a number of different views simply tap on one of the options. However, making Genius mixes is simpler if you view your music as Songs

Refresh
Clicking Refresh will update the tracks that make up your playlist

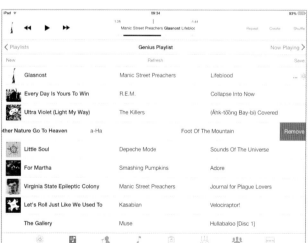

03 You will see that a new option called Genius has been added to the bottom of the interface. Tap on this to see the playlist that Genius has lovingly pieced together for you. Tap on the play button on the cover of the playlist to start listening to it.

04 Tap on the Playlists tab at the bottom of the screen, it will display all of the songs that have been compiled for you. From here you are able to save the playlist, or tap 'Refresh' if you want to add any more songs to the mix. Your playlist will now be up and running.

Purchase an iBook

Learn how to buy an iBook and open up to a whole world of digital books, revolutionising the way you read

O ne of the reasons for the iPad's existence is to take on Amazon's Kindle. The iPad obviously has a number of advantages over the Kindle in that it can do a great deal more than a dedicated device, but on a purely ebook-reading scale, the iPad is still one of the most advanced out there. What's more is that Apple already

has a tried and tested way to deliver ebooks directly to its device: the iTunes Store. However. Apple hasn't just bundled the books into that system, it's created a separate space for these so that users can be sure of what they are downloading.

iBooks is a fantastic resource on your iPad, holding all your ebooks and giving you access to the

custom-built iBooks Store to make purchases. The system is simple, although you may need to download the iBooks app from the App Store to kick things off. This tutorial will take you through your first download from iBooks so you can get a feel for the system. It's then up to you to resist buying a library's worth of content on each visit!

iBooks Purchase a book

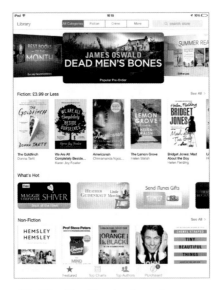

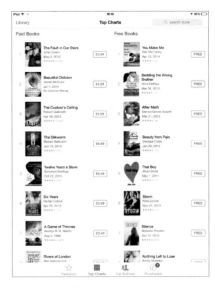

01 Find the iBooks icon on your Home screen, tap it, and once it's loaded, you will be presented with blank shelves. To purchase your first book, hit the 'Store' button at the top left. You'll soon find your shelves all filled up!

02 The iBooks Store is very much like the App Store or the iTunes Store. Books are categorised and searchable, and everything is charted so that you can see what is selling best, but you can also search for specific authors.

03 The 'Featured' section displays all of the latest releases of significance and you can also tap on 'Top Charts' at the bottom of the screen to see which titles are currently popular. It also shows the prices next to the books.

See All
Use the 'See All' button in order to get a bigger list from any given section. It's the same system that's used on the App Store

Promo perfection
Again, like the App Store, books are picked by Apple to be featured on the front of the Store. This positioning increases their sales no end, as you can imagine

Tabs at the bottom
At the bottom of the interface there are four tabs, which will help you navigate through the Store and also see what you have already bought previously

Easy navigation
Navigating through the Store with your fingers is easy. Tap buttons to see more and tap individual books in order to get more information

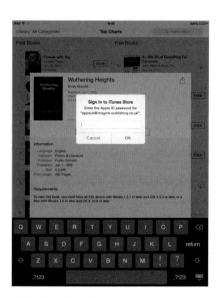

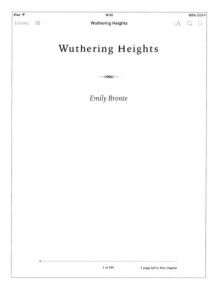

04 Like the App Store, there are a huge number of free books. These tend to be the classics, so you can go ahead and get great content for nothing. Tap on the 'Free' button and then tap 'Get Book'.

05 You'll now be prompted to enter your iTunes account password to authorise the download. Once you've done this and tapped the 'OK' button, the book will start downloading, and will be available to you shortly.

06 Your new books will now appear on the bookshelf and you'll see a progress bar as they download. Once downloaded, the book will become available to read at your leisure. Start collecting and fill up those shelves!

Get to know iBooks

Having an eBook reader on the iPad is very cool, so here's how to customise it to your liking

Despite the conjecture, if you've actually used the iPad you'll know full well that it's much more than just a large iPod touch. The size really does make it feel like you're holding a full-blown computer in your hands, and no other app exemplifies the difference more than iBooks. When you're reading a book on the iPad it feels natural, it's easy to do, and we are certain that we'll be doing a lot more reading now that it's so simple to carry books around with

us. The beauty of the iPad interface means that making changes to the way iBooks looks is very, very simple. Users can opt to make text bigger, change the font and alter the brightness of the book without having to leave the page they are reading. Try doing the same three operations on an iPhone and see how many times you have to leave and return to the page you are reading. iBooks is exceptional, so follow our tutorial on how to get more from the reading experience.

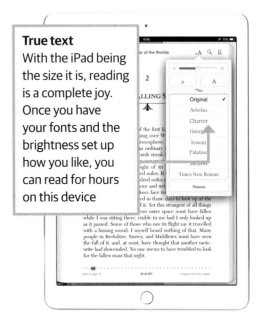

True text
With the iPad being the size it is, reading is a complete joy. Once you have your fonts and the brightness set up how you like, you can read for hours on this device

iBooks Font, size and brightness

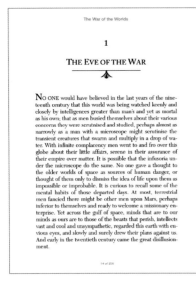

01 Open the iBooks app and then tap on the cover of a book on your shelf that you would like to read. The page is presented as if it were a real book, but by tapping on the screen you'll find options at the top and bottom.

02 You can navigate from the contents page to a chapter by tapping on it, and once you have been reading a while, you can head straight to your own bookmarks within the pages themselves, for super-quick navigation.

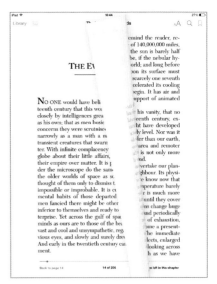

03 You can flip through pages by dragging from the right-hand side to the left, where you'll see the cool page-curl animation. Or use the less cool but more functional tap on the right-hand side to skip to the next page.

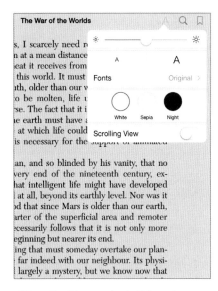

04
Tap on the 'aA' font button at the top to access the menu where you can alter the book's font and text size. Tap the big 'A' to increase font size and the small one to decrease it, depending on how easy you find the text to read.

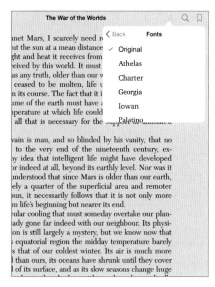

05
If you're not keen on the font used, you can change the font type. Tap the 'Fonts' button and then pick from the available options that are listed in the pop-out window. The selection should provide an alternative that suits you.

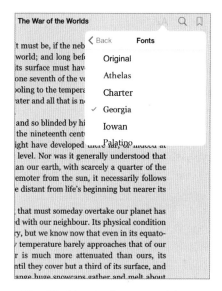

06
Tap the font you wish to select and a tick will appear next to it. As with all the other changes you can make to the appearance of a book within iBooks, they happen instantly, and you can select another one if you wish.

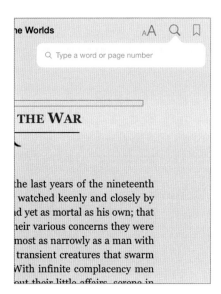

07
Tap on the magnifying glass icon to bring up a search field. Every book on the iBook Store is fully indexed so you can instantly find individual words in a book – invaluable for textbooks and following complicated plots!

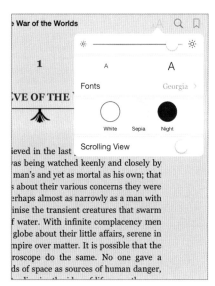

08
Tap on the sunshine icon to bring up brightness settings of the book. This only affects the levels within iBooks and doesn't translate to the rest of the iPad, so you won't have to change it back within other apps.

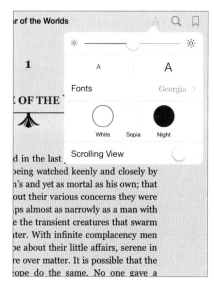

09
Changing the brightness means that you can alter the reading light to whatever is most comfortable for your eyes. The brighter the ambient light, the brighter iBooks needs to be. You can also change the background colour.

Subscribe on Newsstand

The built-in app allows you to subscribe to your favourite magazines and get the new issue on release day

One of the great built-in features of iOS 7 and above is the Newsstand app, which lets you stay on top of all your favourite reading with ease. This app enables you to create a personal magazine library, and has its own dedicated store for you to purchase and download from. The excitement for Newsstand stems from the fact that it means new developers have started afresh on their tablet publications, providing a better reading experience for iPad users. The other big positive with Newsstand is that you can set up subscriptions to your favourite magazines, so you never miss an issue, and have each one accessible to you anywhere in your Newsstand.

More and more magazines are becoming available via Newsstand and the App Store, so the amount of choice is growing constantly, each publication trying to stand out from the crowd with interactive features and extra content. Setting up a subscription is a simple process and a good way to get your bearings should you be new to iOS.

Newsstand Purchase a subscription

01 Tap the Newsstand icon to open up the app and see your library shelves. This is where all your downloaded items will be displayed. It's probably empty, but this will soon start changing as you start subscribing.

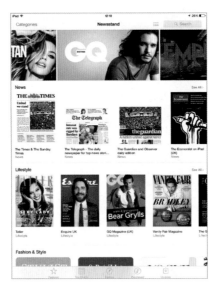

02 To start your magazine search, tap the 'Store' button at the top-right of the Newsstand display. This will take you to the dedicated Newsstand wing of the App Store, where many magazines will be available to you.

03 Here you can browse through all the magazines on sale – either using the various breakdowns provided by the Store, or tapping on 'Featured' at the bottom of the screen and searching the store.

Featured titles
At the top of this page is the animated Featured window, where a selection of the most popular titles are displayed. This is by far the best place to start browsing for interesting apps

Search
If you want to search the store, you can hit any of the buttons at the bottom of the screen to see the Search bar appear

Menu tabs
Along the bottom of the screen you have various tabs to help you navigate, including charts of the bestselling apps, apps popular in your area, and apps you've previously purchased.

Info
When you find a magazine that you want, don't just tap Install; instead tap the icon and get the extra info, including reviews and cost of each issue

04 Once you've found the title you were after, tap Install and enter your iTunes password to download it for free to Newsstand, where you can access back issues and set up your preferred subscriptions.

05 You can now tap the magazine to enter its personal library. You can buy individual issues, or tap the 'Subscribe' icon to see what options and deals are on offer before purchasing.

06 Once you've chosen your subscription and entered your password, the latest issue will become available in the magazine's library. Tap it to download, and start reading. The magazine will stay available to you after use.

Family Sharing organiser
Family Sharing only needs to be set up by one person in the household. When setting up, they will send out invitations to all of the other family members

Accepting invitations
When an invitation has been sent out, the recipient must open it to view it and then accept, after which time they will be added and listed under the Family Sharing settings

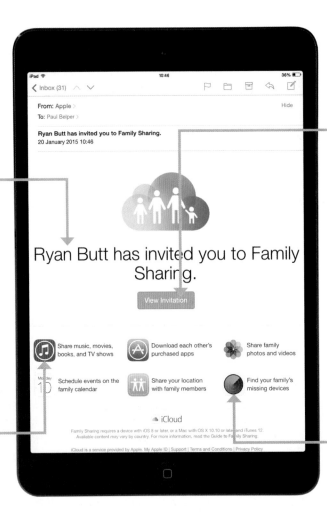

Many benefits
As you will discover, family members who are linked together can share iTunes media, schedule events on the family calendar and more

Find missing devices
One of the most useful aspects of this service is that if a family member loses their device in the house, the organiser can track it and command it to emit a sound

Learn to set up Family Sharing

How to link family members to one account so that all downloaded media can be shared between devices and much more

Family Sharing is a new way to access content from your iPad. Up to six accoutns can share all the different types of iTunes purchases that have been made within the set up family. This service is set up by one family member, known as the organiser, and once set up, all of the family purchases are paid for with the same credit card. This means that young children won't be able to make purchases without the organiser's approval and all of the content can be shared between all of the family members linked to the account.

There are numerous other benefits from using this service; you can share photos quickly and easily within the household, mark up events on a central family calendar and even help track down missing devices. Once set up, family members get instant access to each other's downloaded content without the need to share Apple IDs and passwords. When family members try to buy new content, a permission alert will notify the organiser who can then approve or deny the request.

Settings Get Family Sharing working on your iPad

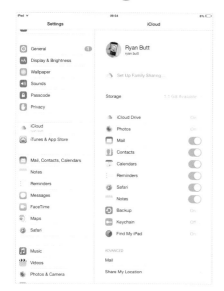

01 Launch the Settings app from your Home screen and scroll down the categories in the column on the left until you come to the iCloud section. Tap on this and you will see the option to Set Up Family Sharing at the top.

02 Tap on the Set Up Family Sharing option followed by Get Started. Now sign in using the Apple ID that you wish to use in order to share iTunes, iBooks and App Store purchases throughout your family.

03 You will have to check the payment method that you wish to use to authorise all iTunes, iBooks and App Store purchases in your household, or enter payment details if they aren't already linked to your Apple ID.

04 The next step involves sharing your location with all family members using Messages and the Find My Friends app. This isn't an essential step to completing the process, so you can tap on Not Now if you prefer.

05 Now the basics have been put in place, you will be taken back to the Settings screen to start adding family members by entering their name or email address. An invitation will be sent and, when accepted, the member will join.

06 From the Family Settings screen of the organiser, you can tap on the names of attached family members to grant/revoke certain app-buying privileges or remove people from the Family Sharing circle.

Design a document

Apple's Pages takes the mobile word-processing experience to a whole new level

Pages is not like most word processors – it combines the most used features in an interface which includes very few icons. Getting to know the app is not difficult, although it does help to understand where the main functions reside in order to get you started, and doing so will open up the power within. Despite the rather sparse interface, it is packed with formatting options and clever little tricks that make previously tiresome manoeuvres a thing of the past. The included templates are completely customisable, which enables you to get creating in no time at all.

Not all specific needs are catered for, such as a word count, but Apple has done a good job of defining the most used functions that people need and being able to share your creations without touching a desktop is another advantage. You can even decide which format to save these documents in and, best of all, if you have iCloud enabled then you can sync your pages wirelessly between devices.

Pages Create stunning documents on the move

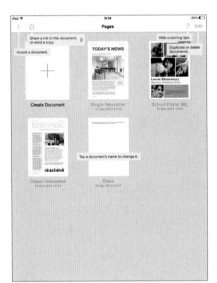

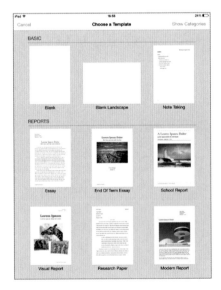

01 The first step is to search for Pages in the App Store, if your iPad came with iOS 7 or iOS 8 preinstalled then it is completely free. The first time you visit the App Store you will be prompted to get it.

02 Pages is so obviously visual in the way it is designed that you could just have a wander around the icons and start typing. If you tap the '?' at the top of the screen at any time, it will display some useful tips.

03 In the first screen, tap the '+' icon at the top and then tap 'New document'. This will bring up a screen with numerous templates on. You can choose anything from a blank page to a party invitation or newsletter.

Document handling
Your completed documents are never far away. A tap of the 'My Documents' icon will bring up a page showing all of your saved work. Each document is saved automatically after every change

Extra formatting
Simply tap the brush icon to access extra formatting features such as bullet points, subtitles and headings. The options automatically change if you have an image highlighted

All the standards
All of the standard formatting options such as bold, italics and underline are easily accessible from the top bar. Highlight a word and click an icon for the desired effect

Easy image manipulation
Once inserted, images can be resized, moved and even twisted to the position you need. The words will automatically move to around them and into the right position

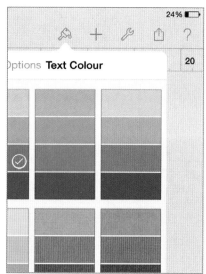

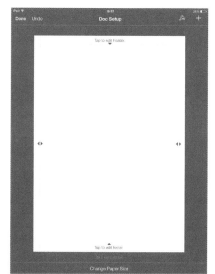

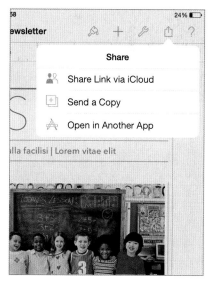

04 Type a few words and then check the formatting options at the top. Select words by tapping and holding, at which point you can use the icons to format the text. Tap the paintbrush icon for more options.

05 Other options include a document setup wizard, defined by the top-right spanner icon and a quick tap of the picture icon lets you insert an image into your document. You can also add in text boxes and shapes.

06 You never need to save your work as you go because Pages does it whenever a change is made to a document, but you can export it to PDF, Pages or Word format and send by email with the tap of one icon.

Make a spreadsheet

Use the versatile Numbers app to create serious or silly spreadsheets to suit all tastes and requirements

Spreadsheets are a part of everyone's lives these days and have taken on multiple roles in business and at home. Most spreadsheet programs tend to focus on the business side because this is where they are mainly used, but spreadsheets have myriad other uses that aren't often explored or understood.

Numbers puts multiple uses front and centre with special templates built in and also brings a new way of working to the mobile user. However, the interface and function locations may feel alien to those that have used Excel for a long time and so a short introduction will help you to get to grips with the app quickly.

There are a lot of functions built in to Numbers and some of these are not obvious, so take a look at these simple steps to start number-crunching straight away.

In this tutorial we take you through the basic steps to set started with Numbers, from entering your first formula to adding charts and formatting.

Numbers Explore the power of this spreadsheet app

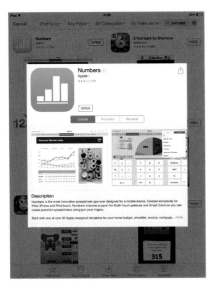

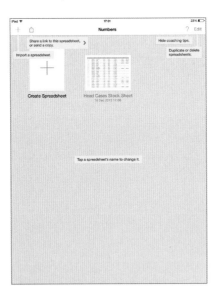

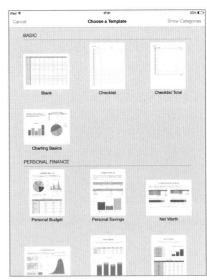

01 If your iPad came with iOS 7 or iOS 8, Numbers is available to download for free from the App Store – so it's well worth taking time to grab it, even if you only need spreadsheets on the odd occasion.

02 When you first open Numbers, you'll be taken to the user manual. It is suggested you read it all. If you find yourself in need of help at a later date tap the '?' and a host of helpful tips shall be displayed on the screen.

03 Tap the '+' icon at the top and select the 'New Spreadsheet' option. You will now be offered a choice of pre-formatted templates which includes everything from a blank spreadsheet to a mortgage calculator.

04 For the purpose of this tutorial, choose the blank template option in the top-left corner and double-tap an empty cell. This brings up a dialog with four icons for numbers, date/time, text and formulas.

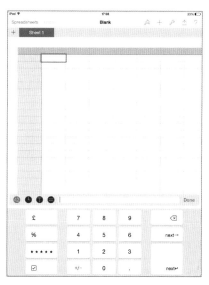

05 Tapping any of the icons brings up a dialog with shortcuts pertinent to the data that you want to input. For example the number icon will bring up a number pad plus a percentage button and so on.

06 Once you've understood where each function resides you can now do something with your content. Tap the '=' icon and you can choose from a wide range of simple functions that will pop up.

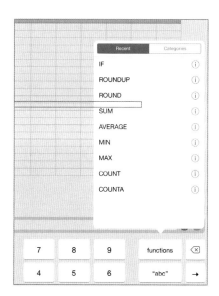

07 The functions button is a window with some serious capability and includes categories of advanced functions such as Trigonometric, Engineering and Statistical. Tap your requires function to input it.

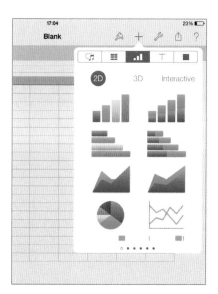

08 Once you have your basic data built you can tap the picture icon in the top-right and insert photos, tables and shapes which will help to make the data more visual. Select and personalise what you need.

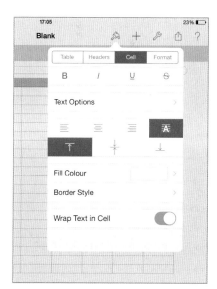

09 Numbers is touch only and this will present problems at first, but the more you practise the more natural it begins to feel. The interface looks simple, but it hides a huge range of options that you'll come to find essential.

Get more from iCloud Drive

Automatically save files on an iOS 8 device and access files from a PC or Yosemite-enabled Mac

The iCloud Drive lets you sync files across multiple iOS devices and computers. It goes beyond the regular iCloud service since it not only allows you to create and save documents in Pages on your iPad and then open them in Pages on a Mac, for instance, it also allows other apps to easily access those files. Files created by one app are no longer restricted to that app alone.

This means you could start creating a drawing in one app, finish it in another and then use it in a presentation. Before, you would have to save it to the Camera Roll, import it, and save it again as a separate image. Now one file is needed which is automatically updated when changes are made, vastly improving your workflow.

Before you upgrade, though, it\s important to note that iCloud Drive is only compatible with iDevices running iOS 8, Macs with Yosemite installed and Windows 7, 7.1 or 8 PCs. If you need to sync with any other or older devices, then it's best that you don't upgrade to Drive just yet.

iCloud Drive Save files to iCloud

01 If you skipped over the option to activate iCloud Drive when you installed iOS 8 onto your iPad, then head over to Settings>iCloud and tap iCloud Drive to activate the service. It uses your Apple ID.

02 Any apps that are using your iCloud Drive are listed in the app's settings. You can turn off access to specific apps if you wish, but recommend all backups, otherwise the apps will automatically upload files.

03 At the bottom of the iCloud Drive settings page you'll see the option to Use Cellular Data (Mobile Data on British English devices), which allows data to transfer to iCloud Drive using your mobile phone plan.

The iCloud structure
There is no iOS 8 iCloud app so the only way to see the structure is through another app – in our case Numbers. Files continue to be stored within their own app space

Numbers and Pages
When you create a file in Apple's own suite of Numbers, Pages or Keynote, it will be saved into iCloud Drive from where it can be easily picked up via iCloud.com or the equivalent Mac apps

Cross-use
Regardless of how the folders are structured, though, the idea is that one app should be able to pull in compatible files from another. So a document or spreadsheet should be universally available across apps if compatible

Storage space
As you fill iCloud Drive with more files, you may run out of space. Go to Settings> iCloud> Storage>Manage Store> Change Storage Plan to buy more (you can choose from 20GB, 200GB, 500GB and 1TB)

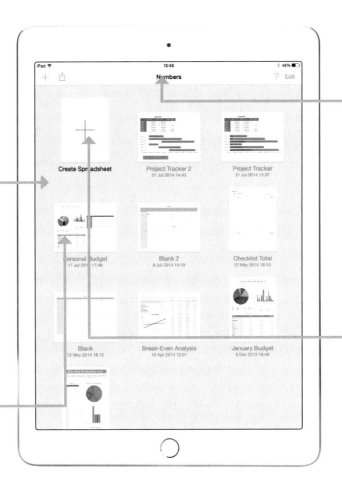

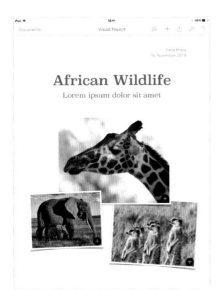

04 There's no standalone iOS 8 iCloud Drive app. Instead, to use the service you must create a file within an iCloud Drive-enabled app, such as Pages or Keynote, for it to automatically save to your Drive.

05 When browsing files, any that are stored in your iCloud Drive which aren't on your device have a downward arrow. Tap it to open and store on your iPad. If you take them off you'll be able to download them again.

06 Any changes you make to a document will now be replicated in iCloud Drive, so you no longer need to make numerous copies of a single file to keep everything up-to-date. That's rather handy.

Send your files with AirDrop

AirDrop can help you to share and receive files with anyone who happens to be in the vicinity

irDrop is designed to let you send and receive files to any compatible phone or tablet that is within close proximity to you. This means that you can share files in a couple of seconds with anyone who is happy to receive it and, of course, it works the other way around too. The process really is extremely simple,

and – more importantly – very reliable. Multiple file types are supported and you can share many files at the same time, and even large files are supported within the technology. The idea is that no real set up is required and that the process feels almost invisible in use. You may not use it often, but when you need it everything

will work seamlessly and without any fuss at all. It is very secure and you always have control over which files you are dealing with.

Permission has to be given to receive files and enough information is available so that you know who you are sharing with and what it is they are sending or you are sending them. Let's get started.

AirDrop Share files with AirDrop

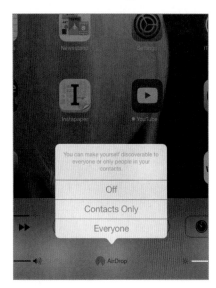

01 Pull up the Control Centre and then tap the small AirDrop icon. A menu shall appear and you will be offered a choice of options: 'Off', 'Contacts Only' or 'Everyone'. Choose 'Everyone' to get started.

02 The icon will turn white which means that AirDrop is now available to send and receive files to your device provided someone else is close to you. It works a lot like bluetooth devices in this manner.

03 Choose a file to send, such as a photo, and then tap the share icon that's located in the bottom-left. You should see an icon showing who is near. Select the person you would like to send your files to.

File types
Many different file types are supported in AirDrop. Some will open automatically and others will offer choices for which app to use

A large space
The sharing space allocated to AirDrop is generous. Tap anywhere to send a file or to see warning message if something goes wrong

A visual indicator
If someone is within range and has AirDrop activated you will see a different icon replace the AirDrop one. Simply tap to send

Make your choice
You can choose how you want to use AirDrop here. Turn it on and off or send to specific contacts or anyone in range

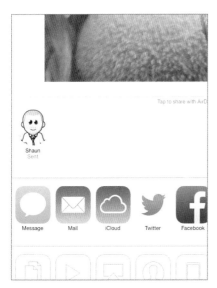

04 Once the recipient has accepted the file and it has been sent through, you shall be able to see the status of the file beneath their name. You will be able to track when the file is then 'sent', or observer any issues.

05 If someone sends you a file, a notification will pop up no matter what you are currently doing on the iPad. Tap 'Accept' in order to receive the files. You have the option to decline unwanted files if you so wish.

06 Depending on the type of file received, it may open automatically in the correct app. Photos for example will open immediately in the Photo app. Others you may have to select the correct app to open with.

Stream content with AirPlay

You can turn your iPad into your home media hub by streaming audio and video to other devices in your home. Here's how

While it's great to be able to carry your favourite films, photos and music with you on your iPad wherever you go, let's be honest: the joy is a personal one, as the iPad's speakers and screen are hardly built for sharing with a wider audience.

Or at least it would be without the iPad's killer feature: AirPlay. It allows you to stream your iPad's music, video and images wirelessly across a local network.

The only extra you need to use AirPlay is a compatible device to stream your iPad's content to. This could be an AppleTV, AirPlay-enabled stereo speakers – of which there are several on the market – or an AirPort Express wireless base station, which

comes with a socket that enables it to connect to a home stereo system. A button tap is all it takes to free your audio and video and watch films on the big screen, or listen to your music collection on your best speakers. No wires required.

> "The iPad's killer feature AirPlay allows you to stream your iPad's music, video and images wirelessly across a local network"

AirPlay Set up your AirPlay connection

01 AirPlay works over a local Wi-fi network, so check that your iPad and the device you're streaming to are on the same network. You can set this up on the iPad by tapping Settings and choosing the 'Wi-fi' option. If your network is secured, you will need to enter its password.

02 When your devices are properly connected, start playing the media on the iPad that you want to stream to another device. When you play a movie or a song on your iPad tap the AirPlay icon (a hollow rectangle with a solid triangle) that appears on the media controller.

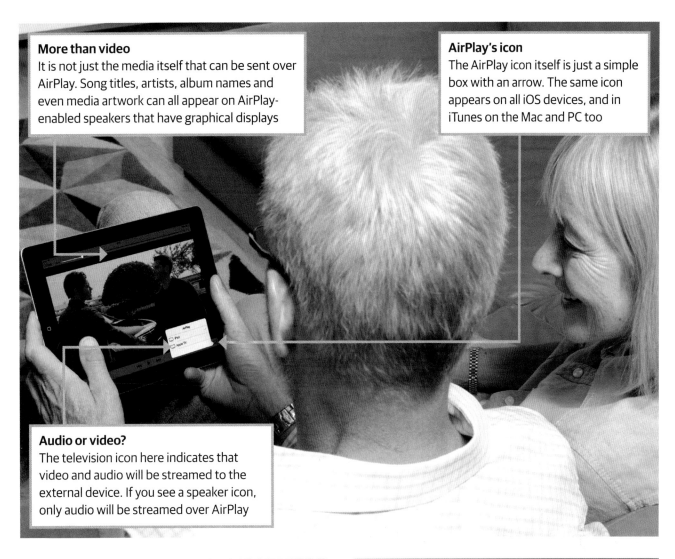

More than video
It is not just the media itself that can be sent over AirPlay. Song titles, artists, album names and even media artwork can all appear on AirPlay-enabled speakers that have graphical displays

AirPlay's icon
The AirPlay icon itself is just a simple box with an arrow. The same icon appears on all iOS devices, and in iTunes on the Mac and PC too

Audio or video?
The television icon here indicates that video and audio will be streamed to the external device. If you see a speaker icon, only audio will be streamed over AirPlay

03 When you tap the AirPlay icon, a pop-up menu will appear, offering a choice of AirPlay-enabled devices. The currently selected output displays a tick next to it, and it should be your iPad. Tap the name of the device that you would like to stream to.

04 Unfortunately, you are not able to watch the same video in two places at the same time. Once you have selected another output device from the list, the video or audio is sent there within just a couple of seconds. The iPad's screen will then go blank!

Join Twitter and get tweeting

Get onto the phenomenon that is social media and connect with friends in an exciting way

It's not an exaggeration to say that Twitter is a social phenomenon. Whether you are already a part of the tweeting community or you are new to it, you will be aware of the terms 'hashtag' and 'trending topics'. And if you aren't, by the end of this tutorial, you will be! In iOS 8, Twitter comes as a part of the package. When you first set up you are given the option to connect your Twitter account or to join the social media service.

Whilst you may think of Twitter as 140 characters of mindless chatter, there is a lot more to it than that. It helps keeps you connected with friends and family, whilst also allowing you to keep up with what's going on in the world around you.

In this tutorial we show you how to create an account, follow your favourite Twitter feeds and start sending your own tweets and direct messages to your followers. Discover the world of Twitter and start joining in and doing more than you ever thought of before.

Twitter Learn the essentials of Twitter life

01 Head over to the App Store. Search for Twitter and tap Get>Install. Once it has installed, tap Open and it will take you to the app. You will be greeted with the home screen and the option to Sign Up or Log In.

02 If you are new to Twitter, tap on Sign Up and it will take you to the Sign Up screen. Fill out your details and choose your Twitter handle (what you will be known as). If you already have an account, simply log in.

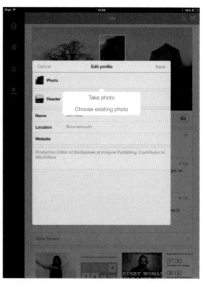

03 Fill out details such as your Bio; this is what people will read on your profile. To add a picture, tap the picture area and select one from your photos. This will appear next to your tweets on other people's feeds.

Follows you
You can see if a user follows you back by the words Follows You next to their Twitter name

Follow a user
To follow somebody, tap on the Follow button under their profile header. Once you have followed them it will read Following instead. To Unfollow, all you need to do is tap the button again.

Statistics
You can see how many tweets, followers or followees a user has. Tap them to view the list of names.

Favourite & retweet
You can favourite a tweet so you can find it again easily. If a user tweets something you wish to share, then you can hit the Retweet button to share with your own followers.

04 To send a new tweet, tap on the quill square in the top-right corner of the screen. Type in your tweet and tap the Tweet button. This will now appear on your feed. You can add links to websites and pictures.

05 To view your notifications – replies, favourites and retweets – tap on the Notification tab on the left-hand side of the screen. In order to reply, tap the arrow, or simply type '@ (username)' to talk to another user.

06 The Discover tab is where you will find all of the trending topics and popular tweets from the people you follow. There will be suggestions of people to follow and the most popular topics, or 'Trending topics'.

Facebook your friends & family

Be sociable with your friends and family on the biggest social network going – never miss a thing again!

Facebook is everywhere. From online trends making their roots in the pages of the popular networking site, to news breaking to the masses using the system.

Posting to Facebook is simple. You can easily share any aspect of your life that you want, from pictures of a recent project or

holiday, to keeping your friends and family updated on your life in general. You can post whatever you want to share and choose exactly who you share it with.

Facebook even has the ability for you to link your interests with pages from a wide range of subjects from TV shows to the more obscure hobbies. Even film

quotes get pages of their own, so there is something for all. Here we will show you how to find what you are looking for to formulate a news feed that is perfect for you.

So connect with your friends, like their pictures, comment on their statuses and generally keep up-to-date with what is going on in your social circles.

Facebook Connect with your friends

01 Joining Facebook is simple. Download the app from the App Store. Open the app. If you already have an account, simply sign in. If you don't, tap Sign up for Facebook at the bottom of the screen and follow the instructions.

02 Once you have signed up and added your first profile image, you will be taken to your News Feed which will fill up with your friends' statuses and pictures. To view your profile, tap your name in the top-right corner.

03 To add new friends, tap in the search box at the top of the screen and type in your friend's name. People with mutual friends will appear at the top, as will people with similar locations or job. Tap on Add Friend.

Check in
To share your current locations with your friends tap Check In, search for the place and tap Post

Unfollow
If you are finding that your friends are sharing posts that you do not wish to see, tap on the down arrow next to the post and then chose Unfollow. That way you can still be friends, without seeing posts that don't interest you

Like
You will have heard the term 'Like' when it comes to Facebook. To do so, just tap on the thumbs up beneath the status or photo. Unlike in the exact same way

Comment
To leave a comment on a photo or status, tap on Comment beneath the object and simply type in your reply, then tap Post

04 One of the main features is status updates. To share something with your friends, simply tap on Status and type out your update. You can add photos, tag friends, and add locations to your posts at the bottom.

05 Tap on Photos at the top. You will have to allow photo access. Tap on the photos you wish to add and tap Done. At the bottom you can add to albums, and tag friends to your post. When done tap Post.

06 To find your interests on Facebook, simply search for them in the top bar and you will be given the options. Tap on the name of the page to go to it, then tap on the Like thumb beneath their user picture to like the page.

Essential iPad apps

Get the most out of your iPad with a wide range of apps to make virtually every aspect of your life easier!

Now that you have spent a lot of money on an iPad, you'll want to get the maximum return from your investment – and this is where apps come in. They say there is an app for everything and this, as you'll soon discover, is very true. We will showcase a variety of apps that can actually help you in your day-to-day life and make life much easier. Whether it's staying in touch with your family or friends, keeping your mind and body exercised or just giving the grandchildren something to do when they come to visit, we have hand-picked a varied array of apps to help in each scenario.

As you'll soon discover, buying an iPad was one of the best decisions you have ever made because it opens up a variety of possibilities and will help you relax and unwind, get up and go, look after your house and organise your dream holiday. And that's just the tip of the iceberg…

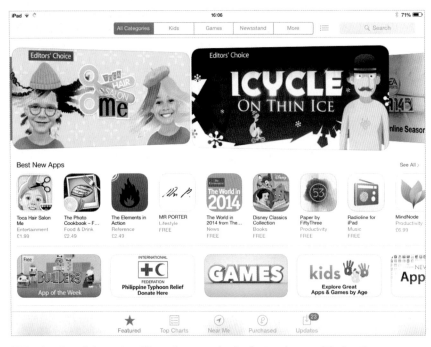

■ The App Store is home to millions of apps, and we've featured some of the best here

"We will showcase a variety of apps that can actually help you in your day-to-day life and make life much easier"

5 essential apps

Skype for iPad

Through Skype's intuitive interface you can send unlimited text messages and talk face-to-face with your friends and family for free. It truly is the next best thing to being there in the room with them!

Facebook

The world's most popular social network is a fun and casual way to stay in touch with your friends and family and get regular status reports on what everyone is up to. You can also share photos and video through this service.

Pinterest

Pinterest is a great little app where you can collect and share your interests and hobbies. Collect, or "pin" recipes, DIY projects, fitness tips, or just beautiful pictures for later use, or share them with your friends.

Talkatone

If you like to chat for hours on the phone to your friends and family then you can completely eradicate all costs with this app. You can make the calls through your iPad instead and not pay a penny for them.

Google+

Like Facebook, Google+ is a social network, but with this one you can split your friends and family into different groups (so you aren't posting to everyone at once) and organise your own meetings and events easily.

Keep in touch

One of the ways in which iPads have enriched our lives is by making it easier to communicate with family and friends. Through easy-to-use apps, we can now converse with people as if they are actually stood in the same room thanks to the video technology that the iPad's front and rear-facing cameras afford us. Of course, email and social networking apps are good for showing others that we're thinking about them and providing general overviews as to our thoughts and feelings. But if you want a really good chat with a personal touch then there are plenty of good, free apps that allow you to talk, text or converse face-to-face with your friends and family – so it feels as natural as being in the same room as them, even if you are on the opposite side of the world!

■ Enjoy full-screen, face-to-face video conferencing with Skype's excellent app

■ Share your feelings and photos with your friends and family with Facebook

■ Instead of subjecting everyone to your posts, Google+ splits audiences into groups

■ Simply select a person from your contacts list and then you can chat to them for free

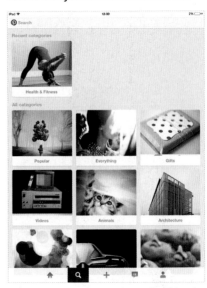

■ Use Pinterest as your personal cookbook, fitness manual, or as a social network

■ Club Penguin lets children explore a whole new world of fun

■ The Cbeebies Magazine app features garish, interactive fun for young children

Apps for grandchildren

If you have been left in charge of the grandchildren over half term then you needn't worry about not having toys, colouring books or DVDs to hand because your iPad is a perfect way to keep them enthralled while buying you some much-needed peace and quiet.

With such a wide and diverse range of apps available, many of which are free, iPads are fun for all the family, and can certainly amuse children of all ages for hours on end. Obviously different children are into different things, but with plenty on offer to fuel creativity, intrigue and intellect, apps can be both fun and educational, as the following examples are testament to. Just remember to go to your iPad's General Settings, tap on 'Restrictions' and ensure that in-app purchases are turned off and a password is required to download new apps – you'd wouldn't want them unwittingly bankrupting you!

■ Children will have great fun interacting while learning plenty of prehistoric facts

■ In Video Star, Kids can create their own pop videos and make you watch them!

■ Kids can give any photo a new personality with Facegoo HD's assorted range of effects

5 essential apps

CBeebies Magazine

The iPad is a great way to read – and good for the environment too. Pretty much every comic has an app version, including this offering, which is ideal for young kids thanks to its engaging stories and interactive games.

Dinosaur Zoo

Fun, engaging and educational, this app lets children build their own dino enclosure, learn plenty of facts about their characteristics and, best of all, interact with the snarling creatures. Careful they don't make them angry, though!

FaceGoo HD

Using photos imported from your iPad, or a few stock images, kids can have great fun distorting them with their fingers and adding all manner of wacky embellishments, such as oozing spots and comedy specs.

Club Penguin

Your grandchildren will love this virtual island full of games and adventures. Club Penguin is a multiplayer community that lets children create their own personal penguin, make friends, adopt pets, and collect items.

Video Star
A proven hit with kids and teenagers, this free app makes children the stars of their own pop videos thanks to an array of cool special effects and free songs. It's easy to use with professional-looking results.

5 essential apps

The Tower

Build a tower as high as possible, sounds simple, right? The Tower turns this simple idea into an addictive game. Tap the screen as building blocks slide in to put them in place and keep stacking as the game speeds up!

Scrabble

This classic boardgame is just as fun on your iPad, and even comes with a few extra options. You can play online against people all over the world, as well as friends who also have the app, or play against the computer.

Crossword+

If you enjoy exercising your grey matter with a good crossword over a cup of coffee then this free app helpfully generates as many as you'll ever need – and you can tailor it to suit the level of challenge you require.

Sudoku

The popular number placement game works well on iPad with plenty of variants on offer. This free offering features a point system, a time limit and, should you wish to compete, an online leaderboard.

Solitaire

This classic card game also lends itself well to iPad, with crisp visuals and a slick control system in which you can drag the cards around the screen using your finger. It's still as addictive as ever, just easier to play.

■ Play an old fashioned game of Scrabble anywhere, against anyone

Games

The iPad can be used as an enthralling games console, with what seems like hundreds of thousands of games for when you just want to unwind and have fun. Naturally there are games to suit all ages and preferences but it excels in the puzzle category, with a great many crossword, quiz and number-crunching apps available to help you relax while giving your brain – and at times your fingers – a thorough workout.

You won't have to worry about spending a fortune on apps either as the majority of the games featured here are totally free, the only downside being that there may be adverts visible on screen while you play – but these are unintrusive and

■ Align the building blocks for your Grecian tower perfectly for extra points

will in no way spoil your enjoyment of the game. So take time out and treat yourself to one or more of these compelling apps to test your grey matter.

■ The free Crossword+ app provides a mental workout whenever you need it

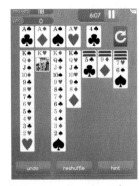

■ Same great game, made even more accessible with your iPad's touch screen

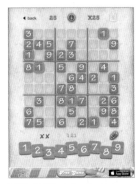

■ Digital Sudoku means you'll never have to fumble around for a pen that works

■ Take all of the stress out of planning a dinner party with this easy-to-use app

■ Take the stress out of your food shopping and buy online through Ocado

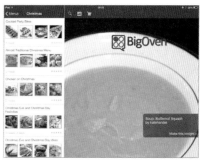

■ Search for dishes, grab the ingredients and follow the easy instructions to prepare the perfect meals

Perfect your cooking

A s we all know, cooking can mean different things to different people. Some like exploring new flavours and trying out exciting new dishes, others see is as a necessity that they would rather do without. Whatever your outlook, your iPad makes for the perfect cooking companion, sourcing you inspiring recipes to wow the guests at a dinner party or helping you rustling up quick and easy meals that taste great in no time at all.

If you have a stand, you can prop your iPad up next to you as you get to work in the kitchen and it'll take up much less space on your worktops than a bulky cookbook and provide all the step-by-step instructions you need to help you prepare top quality food. You can even use your iPad to compile shopping lists to ensure you have everything you need and can then do all your shopping online to prevent you from having to step outside. Bliss!

■ Change4Life's app Smart Recipes goes back to traditional cooking and helps avoid the quick-and-easy nature of modern eating

"Whatever your outlook, your iPad makes for the perfect cooking companion"

■ Browse a wide range of meals and get expert prep tips from Jamie Oliver himself

5 essential apps

BigOven: 250,000+ Recipes and Grocery List

 If you're in need of some culinary inspiration then this app provides thousands of easy-to-follow recipes with step-by-step instructions.

Recipe, Menu & Cooking Planner

 If you're planning on hosting a party then this app provides everything you need to plan your quantities, buy your ingredients and cook your meals thanks to a friendly and easy-to-use interface.

Ocado

 Supermarkets can be stressful places that a lot of us would rather not brave, and with apps like Ocado you don't have to. This app lets you do your shopping online and get everything delivered to your door.

Jamie's 15-Minute Meals

 If you're tired after a long day and don't relish the prospect of slaving over a stove then you'll find a wide range of tasty Jamie Oliver recipes that can be knocked up and served in no time.

Smart Recipes

 As it is sponsored by Change4Life, this app is designed to make healthy eating possible even with a busy modern lifestyle. It includes food plans, cooking tips, and information about healthy eating.

Read in style

Your iPad is a great device for reading on. It's light enough that you can hold it in one hand like a paperback and tailor the reading options – such as screen brightness, size of the font, colour of the text – to suit your needs and the current lighting conditions.

Better still, your device can store thousands of digital books, so you essentially get your very own mini library that you can carry around with you everywhere.

There are a great many cracking reading apps that you can download on the iPad, most of which offer similar features such as easy access to their respective book stores, the option to download sample pages so that you can try before you buy,

thousands of free classic books and automatic syncing, so that all of your recent read pages, bookmarks and notes are updated across your account. What this means is that you can start reading a book on your iPad and then pick up where you left off later on a computer or other mobile device.

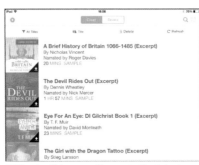

■ The Audible app will narrate the latest bestsellers out loud to you

■ Through Goodreads' simple interface you can discover new books

■ Like most reading apps, Google Play Books lets you easily explore the book

■ Me Books will include all of your old favourites, as well as some new stories

■ The Kindle app you can bookmark pages and look out words in a built-in dictionary

5 essential apps

Audiobooks from Audible

With over 100,000 books available, this app will read your favourite novels aloud, allowing you to enjoy the latest bestseller without you even having to hold your iPad, or even look at it!

Kindle

The free Kindle app provides access to over 900,000 books and all of your last read pages, bookmarks, and notes are synced, so you can pick up where you left off, be it your computer, iPad or Kindle device.

Google Play Books

Google's reading app offers millions of digital books for instant download and features many options to suit your needs, including night-reading mode and voice-over.

Me Books

If you want to read to your grandchildren from your iPad, try Me Books. This app contains all the classic children's tales, but also stories from their favourite TV characters, picture books, and comics.

Goodreads

This app is like a literary social network where recommendations are shared and books are reviewed to help you ensure that the time you invest in your reading is well spent and not wasted on a stinker.

■ Daily Workouts provides expert video guidance to help you keep fit

Stay healthy

As we get older it is important to look after our bodies by watching what we eat and exercising regularly. However, sometimes we need a little extra motivation to do so. Well your iPad can act as the perfect fitness coach and all-round health guru thanks to a variety of great apps.

The Health & Fitness section of the App Store is full of apps to help you with all aspects of your well-being, including workout and running apps that let you tailor your own regimes to suit your needs (and get video tuition to ensure you don't damage yourself!) and apps that monitor your calorie intake so that you can enjoy the benefits of a healthy, lean body. You will also find apps to help you get expert advice and reassurance for any ailments that you have and apps to help you relax and enjoy the many benefits of yoga. We have recommended some of the most well-produced and beneficial apps here.

> "Your iPad can act as the perfect fitness coach and all-round health guru"

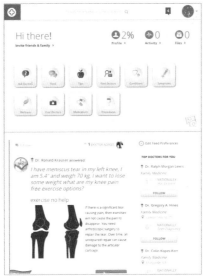

■ Through HealthTap's simple interface you can get expert advice

■ Calorie Counter can help you reach your desired weight through careful monitoring

■ Create your own custom yoga routines with this relaxing and easy-to-use app

■ Walk4Life lets you keep track of all your walking routes

5 essential apps

Calorie Counter and Diet Tracker HD

A great way to lose weight, this app helps you monitor your calorie intake by using your iPad's camera to scan the barcodes of food products to check the contents and plan your diets.

Daily Workouts

This useful app helps you stay in shape by providing daily randomly generated workouts for you to try. You can select a duration and area to focus on and videos are provided to help you get the technique just right.

Daily Yoga

Yoga is a great way to keep you supple and help you relax and this app helps you build your own custom yoga experience, from the training regimes to the soothing music that accompanies your sessions.

HealthTap

There are times when we feel under the weather but don't want to visit the doctors. This app provides answers from over 36,000 doctors, so you can look up your ailments and determine the best course of action.

Walk4Life

Also sponsored by Change4Life, this app lets you log your walks and hikes. It allows you to record distance, speed, and calories burned, and even plots a map for you so you can revisit your routes for your next walk.

5 essential apps

Google Earth

The first step of planning a holiday is deciding where to go. With this you have the whole world in your hands and can jump to any place on the planet and even zoom right in to street level to check out the sights.

KAYAK

This useful app lets you scout out and book accommodation, plane tickets and even hire cars at your chosen holiday destination. It takes all of the stress out of arranging holidays, leaving you free to enjoy them.

TripAdvisor Hotels Flights Restaurants

This app is very useful for finding the best hotels, restaurants and fun things to do wherever you go. You can also use the app to make all of your travel arrangements and read thousands of reviews.

XE Currency

It's easy to get carried away and overspend while on holiday, but this free currency convertor app allows you to quickly see how any foreign currency stacks up against the Stirling and you can use it offline.

Lowcostholidays

Not only does this app let you look up the cheapest options for your desired holidays, it also suggests inspirational ideas and options for low prices, based on your needs or plans. Impromptu trip to Laos, anyone?

Plan the perfect holiday

As holiday trips away don't tend to come around very often, it's important that when you do go away the whole experience is stress-free and relaxing. Armed with a few apps on your iPad, you can do everything from scout out possible holiday locations, book all of your travel arrangements, including flights, hotels and transport for when you arrive at your destination.

There are also several apps available to help you ensure that you don't forget to pack any essential items and make sure that you don't accidentally overspend when you are away on your holiday by providing simple currency convertors that store the very latest rates on your device, so that you can use it even without an internet connection.

Tried and tested by millions of people, the following apps will ensure that every aspect of your dream holiday can be arranged from the comfort of your iPad within minutes, leaving you free to enjoy your holiday without having to worry about a thing.

■ Get instant clarification on how the foreign currencies stack up with XE

■ Explore the world with your fingers and scout out places to visit with Google Earth

■ Through the KAYAK app you can browse and arrange all aspects of your holiday

■ Check TripAdvisor reviews to see if your potential accommodation is up to scratch

■ Let Lowcostholidays suggest a destination for your next trip, based on the occasion

■ TED offers you the latest lectures from the world's most famous intellectuals

■ Fit Brains Trainer features a varied mix of fun games to test your mental agility

Boost your brainpower

As we get older we can enjoy having more time on our hands and what better way to spend this time than by learning new things to expand our minds? Of course, our minds aren't as sponge-like to retaining information as they were when we were younger, but thankfully there are plenty of apps on hand to give our brains a mental workout to help keep them fresh and ticking over.

Your iPad can be a great learning aid and you'll find apps that cover a wide range of topics in the Education section of the App Store that will help to teach you new things and bolster your mental arsenal in preparation for those quiz evenings. You will also find a great many mental training aids that provide fun and engaging questions and puzzles to solve to determine where your mental strengths lie and generally whir your brain into action for the busy day ahead.

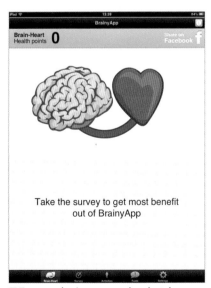

■ Test your brainpower and undertake regular activities in BrainyApp

■ Discover what areas of your brain work the best with The IQ Test's mental agility exam

■ Thanks to a wide range of study materials, you can learn new things with iTunes U

iTunes U

 You're never too old to learn new things and this app provides a vast library of learning materials to enable you to study a wide range of subjects to help expand your mind (and boost your quizzing ability!).

Fit Brains Trainer

This free app provides your brain with a vigorous daily workout to keep it sharp and fully functioning! It features a varied mix of questions to test your mental agility and help improve your brain's performance.

BrainyApp

 This app actually helps you rate and track your brain's health and guide you on how healthy living can help boost your intelligence. You can take the in-app test and carry out regular activities to boost your mind.

The IQ Test

 Through a series of tasks (over 900 questions are available in the app), this is designed to work your mind and test you in 13 different areas of intelligence to reveal your cognizant strengths and weaknesses.

TED

 Take a seat and invite the greatest thinkers of our time into your living room. TED caters for every one of your interests, and offers speeches, talks and seminars on medicine, business, technology, sociology, and many more.

Your iPad FAQs

Having problems with your iPad? Let us guide you through some of the most common tablet troubles that people experience

Freezing iPad

My iPad has frozen. How can I reset it?

You can tell instantly when your iPad crashes. The touchscreen will stop responding and you can't perform any operations. The display may go blank or black. If this happens to you, don't despair. It isn't broken – you just need to kickstart it back into life.

Before you do anything, try turning the iPad off and then back on again by holding the Sleep/Wake button and using the red slider to switch off, then pressing the same button to turn it back on again. In some cases, this will not do anything so you will need to reset it. This is done by pressing the Sleep/Wake button and the Home button at the same time. Hold both for ten seconds. The Apple logo will appear and the iPad is reset.

Step by step – Reset your iPad

Turn iPad off

01 Press and hold the Sleep/Wake button until you see the red slider. Slide this to the right to turn the iPad off and then press Sleep/Wake to turn it back on again.

Reset the iPad

02 If this doesn't work, then it will need a proper reset. Press the Sleep/Wake button and the Home button at the same time and hold it for ten seconds.

Start iPad again

03 The Apple logo will appear. The machine has now been reset and if you wait a few seconds, you will soon see your familiar icons once again.

Lost passcode

I've forgotten my passcode – can I still unlock my iPad?

An iPad is not automatically locked using a passcode. You have to set one yourself. Assuming you have done this and subsequently forgotten the passcode, all is not lost. It is still possible to gain access to your iPad. The only problem is that you will have to restore it to the factory settings in order to do so. What this means is that you will lose any data stored on the tablet. It is therefore vital to ensure that you frequently back up (see page 38).

In order to restore your iPad, you will need to connect it to the computer to which you last synced your device. So, for example, if you always sync your iPad with your home PC, make sure you connect your iPad to that machine. Any data which you have backed up on your computer will be put back on to your iPad if you do this. Crucially, the passcode you've forgotten will not be put back so you are free to input a new one.

Step by step – Reset your iPad from a computer

Connect to computer

01 Connect your iPad to your computer and download and open up iTunes. Click on the Summary tab at the top of the screen and you will be able to see an overview of your iPad.

Restore the iPad

02 In the top box on the Summary page, you will see the version of iOS you have installed. Here you need to click Restore iPad and decide whether to back up the settings.

Restore and Update

03 Having clicked Back Up, your settings will be saved. The iTunes app will then show another prompt box. Click Restore and Update to begin the process of restoring your iPad.

Deleting apps

How can I delete an app from my iPad?

■ In the course of using your iPad, you will download a large number of apps. While you will undoubtedly want to keep many of these, there will be some that you wish to delete. To do this go to the main screens of the iPad – the ones which contain all of the icons of the apps. Find the icon of the app that you do not want to keep. Now tap and hold down on this icon. After a few seconds, all the apps will begin to shake. Next to the installed apps will be an X. By

tapping the X on the icon of the app you wish to delete, you will be able to remove it. A box will appear asking

if you do indeed wish to Delete. Indicate that you do and the app will vanish.

Getting physical

Can I use a physical keyboard rather than the on-screen one?

The simple answer is yes. The on-screen keyboard is great, but if you want to type for long periods, nothing beats a physical keyboard and it seems that Apple is aware of this fact as well.

Pretty much any Bluetooth keyboard can be used with an iPad and a great deal of them are actually tailored for use with the iPad. What you will be after, ideally, is something small and portable to fit in with the lightweight nature of the iPad itself. With a specific iPad keyboard, you will also benefit from keys that allow you to make use of the iPad whether it be to adjust the volume, control media playback, jump to the Home screens or adjust brightness.

Which one you go for depends on how you will use it and how frequently. There are keyboards that are designed to be always connected to the iPad and almost become a part of it, effectively turning the iPad into a laptop, and there are those designed to be taken on and off. Some keyboards are more comfortable than others, but, at the same time, less portable.

"Pretty much any Bluetooth keyboard can be used"

Step by step – Connect a Bluetooth keyboard

Obtain keyboard

01 When you have your Bluetooth keyboard, go to the Settings app on your iPad and select General. Make sure that Bluetooth is turned on. It will look for your keyboard.

Find keyboard

02 Make sure the Bluetooth keyboard is turned on. It will then become recognised within the Bluetooth settings on your iPad. Simply tap the name of the keyboard when it appears.

Type pairing code

03 The iPad will display a pairing code. You will need to type this on the keyboard. If done correctly, the keyboard will be paired with the iPad and you will be able to use the two together.

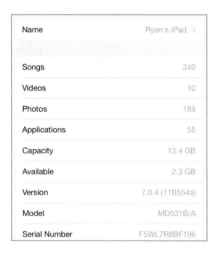

Name	Ryan's iPad >
Songs	340
Videos	10
Photos	189
Applications	55
Capacity	13.4 GB
Available	2.3 GB
Version	7.0.4 (11B554a)
Model	MD531B/A
Serial Number	F5WL7R8BF196

Not enough space
How do I find out how much space I have left on my iPad?

■ The more apps you download, the more pictures you take, and the more videos you store, the less space you will have to play around with.

All of those slices of entertainment, from music to emails, eat away at the storage space on your iPad and it is useful to find out just how much you have used and how much you have left.

Thankfully, it is not difficult to discover the answer. Go to your Settings app and select General then About, which you will see at the top of the screen. In an instant, you will be able to see your iPad's capacity in gigabytes as well as the amount of space available. By tapping Settings and going to General, then Usage, you can narrow down per app and see how much space each app is taking up on your iPad. Perfect for working out what to delete.

Better battery life

How can I make my battery last longer?

Some iPads, according to Apple, have a battery life of up to ten hours. That does not mean you cannot make it last longer, however. The battery will drain only as fast as the demands you place on it, so the common sense approach is to make some small adjustments to your usage. Key to this is ensuring that you still get maximum pleasure from your iPad, too.

Delve into the Settings app on your iPad to start making a difference to your battery's life span, ensuring less frequent recharges. By going to Settings and then Wallpapers & Brightness, for example, you can manage the screen brightness. Turn it down as low as you can without it being uncomfortable and you will save battery power.

Data is a big drainer too. Go to Settings and wi-fi and turn wi-fi off when you are not using it or when you are in an area with poor coverage (your iPad will constantly search for a signal, which will drain the battery). Minimise your use of location services too (Settings, then General, then Location Services). This prevents too many apps from trying to work out where you are, which will affect the battery lifespan.

Push notifications are also bad for your iPad's battery. By preventing apps from pushing information to you when they are not in use, go to the Settings app then the Notification Centre section and turn them off. You can do the same with Mail to prevent you from being notified every time a new email comes through.

Go to Settings

01 By delving into the Settings, you can turn features off that tend to drain the battery when in heavy use. Tap on the Settings icon to call the Settings up.

Push Mail off

02 Tap Mail, Contacts, Calendars and Fetch New Data. Turn Push to Off. By ticking Manually, you can determine when you want emails coming through.

Check fewer emails

03 Do you need to regularly check every email account you have on your iPad? If not, turn an email account off by choosing an unneeded one and turning it off.

19% Charged

Charge iPad
What's the best way to charge my iPad?
■ Although you can charge an iPad by connecting it to a computer via the USB cable, the best way is to use the USB Power Adapter. This is far faster and it also means you don't need to have your computer turned on and active. Apple has recommended that, once a month, you allow your iPad to completely drain, then recharge it to 100 per cent. This keeps the battery healthy.

Capture screenshots
How do I take a screenshot of the iPad?
■ If there is something on the screen that you wish to keep, press and hold the Sleep/Wake button on top of the iPad while pressing the Home button. The screen will flash and you will hear a sound. The screenshot is saved in your Photos app. Tap on the screenshot and you can share it with others via social media or email.

Your iPad glossary

What does it all mean? We guide you through the common features and terms that you're likely to encounter while using your iPad

Apple ID

This is the name and password you use to log in to the various Apple services, such as iTunes, the App Store and iCloud.

Application (app)

An application, or app, is a software program designed to perform one or more functions. Apps can be downloaded from the App Store.

App Store

The App Store is a digital distribution platform for Apple users. Users are able to browse, purchase and download iPad and iPhone apps from the App Store to run on their device.

Dock

A row of icons that can be set to appear at the bottom of your Home screen. The Dock is ever-present as you scroll through screens and allows you to access your favourite apps easily. You can add and remove apps by pressing and holding on an icon until it starts to shake and then dragging it into position.

Game Center

Apple's gaming portal where you can shop for new games, find friends and play against them online or compare high scores.

Gestures

These refer to the finger commands that you perform on your iPad's touch screen to carry out various functions. Multitasking Gestures were added to iOS 5 and later, that let you use five fingers to pinch to reveal your Home screen or swipe up, left or right to reveal your multitasking bar or cycle between open apps.

Gestures jargon:

Tap
● This is the most common and basic gesture to perform on your iPad; it involves tapping the screen with your finger.

Double-Tap
● This involves tapping an object twice in succession. You use this gesture mainly for zooming or highlighting text.

Tap, Hold & Drag
● Some functions, such as highlighting text, copying and pasting require that you tap and hold down on the screen and then drag your finger to select what you want.

Pinch
● To zoom in or to open something, place your thumb and index finger, pinched together, on screen and spread them apart. To zoom out, perform the reverse.

Swipe
● Swiping is one of your primary navigational tools. You perform a left or right swiping motion with your index finger to move through app pages or images in the Photos app, for instance.

Home Button

This is the large circular button on the front of your iPad that you use to quit apps and return to your iPad's home screen.

Home Screen

This is essentially the desktop of your iPad that you see when you boot up or unlock your device. From your home screen, you can launch apps and access your Settings. You can 'pinch' with all five digits to return to the Home screen at any time.

iCloud

iCloud is a free cloud storage and syncing service. With iCloud you can share data, files, music and photographs between devices without the need for manual connecting, syncing and transferring. Go to Settings to log in.

iCloud jargon:

iTunes in the Cloud
● With iCloud, the music you purchase from iTunes appears automatically on all of your devices. You can also download past purchases where you want, when you want.

Photo Stream
● With iCloud, when you take a photo on one device, it automatically appears on all of your Apple-based devices. Photos transferred from a digital camera connected to your Mac will also be pushed to your mobile devices.

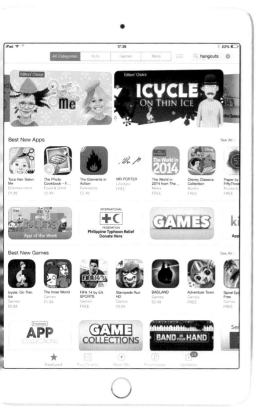

■ You can shop and browse apps by popularity and category at the App Store

Documents in the Cloud
● If you have the same iCloud-enabled apps on more than one device, iCloud automatically keeps your documents up to date across all devices.

iOS
Whereas Macs run on an operating system called OS X (Yosemite being the most recent version), Apple's mobile devices – iPhone, iPad and iPod touch – use iOS. The latest version is iOS 8, which is what you'll find running on all new iPads.

iTunes
This is Apple's flagship digital distribution centre that lets users browse, purchase and download a wide range of digital media, including music, books, movies and television shows. Using an Apple ID, which is set up during activation, users log in

■ iTunes is the ultimate digital marketplace for buying and downloading new music and entertainment for your iPad

and store payment details to make downloading media quick and easy.

iTunes jargon:

Featured
● All of the very latest, most notable music, movies, podcasts and television shows will be showcased under this tab at the front of their respective store windows.

Top Charts
● See what's hot and popular on the iTunes Store by tapping on this tab.

Genius
● A feature that recommends music, films and shows based on what is currently in your library. Genius can also create playlists for you.

iTunes U
● iTunes is also a great source of educational materials, and you'll find a wide range of digital books, videos and podcasts by tapping on the 'iTunes U' link.

Redeem
● Occasionally you may be gifted a product from iTunes in the form of a code. You can click on the 'Redeem' link and input the code to download the product.

Newsstand
This app comes free with iOS and is a place where all of your digital

magazines and newspapers are stored and can be accessed.

Safari
This is Apple's premier web browsing app that comes as standard with all iPad operating systems. The app boasts a wealth of excellent features to make surfing the web an enjoyable and easy experience.

Settings
Accessible from the Dock or Home screen, Settings is where you can tweak your iPad as well as the apps and utilities that make it tick.

Side Switch
This is the small switch on the edge of the iPad that you can assign, via Settings, to act as a mute button or to lock your screen rotation.

Sleep/Wake Button
This is the lozenge-shaped button on top of the iPad that you use to turn your device on and off.

Wi-Fi
Wi-Fi refers to a wireless networking system that allows you to connect to the internet without any cables. You will need access to a wireless router for this to work with your iPad.

■ The Newsstand app is where all of your digital magazines and newspapers are safely stored away

Learn in style

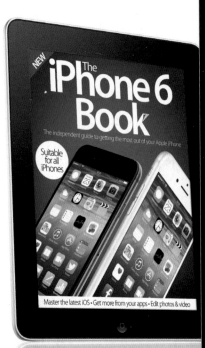

The
Book
Series

Discover more with the Book series' expert, accessible tutorials for iPad, iPhone, Mac, Android, Photoshop, Windows and more

BUY YOUR COPY TODAY

Print edition available at www.imagineshop.co.uk

Digital edition available at www.greatdigitalmags.com

Available on the following platforms

 facebook.com/ImagineBookazines  twitter.com/Books_Imagine